# BEYOND
# FEAR

**www.amplifypublishing.com**

*Beyond Fear: How I Fought the Feds for Six Years—and Won*

**For more information, please contact:**
Amplify Publishing, an imprint of Mascot Books
620 Herndon Parkway #320
Herndon, VA 20170
info@amplifypublishing.com

Library of Congress Control Number: 2020923337

CPSIA Code: PRV0221A
ISBN-13: 978-1-64543-511-2

Printed in the United States

*To my wife, Jayne*

# BEYOND FEAR

HOW I FOUGHT

THE FEDS

FOR SIX YEARS—

AND WON

TED GIOVANIS

# TABLE OF CONTENTS

# AUTHOR'S NOTE

The story you are about to read is one of surprise, intrigue, toil, frustration, love, tragedy, and reward. It begins with filing legal appeals following my discovery that the federal government of the United States erred in its application of a little-known mathematical formula used to calculate Medicare payment rates for hospitals. Amid overwhelming evidence of the error, the government unleashed its lawyers to make false claims, which three judges of the United States Court of Appeals for the D.C. Circuit ultimately—and unanimously—rejected. The recalcitrance was not the fault of political appointees. It was driven by senior career employees who feared that acknowledging the mathematical error might tarnish their retirement prospects. The episode was a stark reminder of the power of the "deep state," by which I mean individuals or a collection of individuals who serve as "career" federal employees—meaning they stay in their jobs irrespective of whether a Republican or a Democrat is president. They are ostensibly nonpolitical, but they can—and will—use the full force of the federal government to manipulate public policy and defend their interests, whether those interests are ideological or personal (or both). They rarely lose—but in this instance they did.

# INTRODUCTION

Wednesday, May 3, 2006, was a day as normal as any other. I was attending to various issues when a client called to ask me a question. He wanted more information about how the Medicare program calculated something called "budget neutrality" (BN), which is a simple way of referring to a complicated process. BN involves making adjustments to the payment rate that is used to reimburse hospitals under Medicare's Inpatient Prospective Payment System, as well as other payment systems, when select payment adjustments are changed. The specific question was about how the area wage index (AWI), which is an adjustment for area wage differences, was budget neutralized.

I had been asked this question several times in the previous year, provoked by a consultant who was telling hospitals, industry representatives, and hospital associations that the Medicare program was incorrectly calculating BN as it related to the AWI. This consultant believed that a change to the data, prompted by removing from the wage data one class of hospitals (known as critical access hospitals), had caused this particular BN calculation to be performed improperly. As a result, he said, hospitals were losing billions in revenue.

Upon each of those previous occasions, my response to clients was the same: Medicare was performing the calculation correctly, and the shortfall was compensated for by the BN calculation as payment rates were adjusted. In other words, there was no shortfall.

I eventually tired of these questions and decided I wanted a definitive clarifying answer. I emailed a professional acquaintance, Mike (not his real name), who at the time was the deputy director of the Division of Acute Care at the Center for Medicare and Medicaid Services (CMS), the federal agency that administers the two programs. I posed an elementary question: How is BN calculated including the relevant data elements?

A little more than three hours later, I received a detailed response from one of his colleagues, Nina (not her real name). While the response confirmed that the consultant was wrong, there was another bombshell buried in the response that would launch me on an odyssey that would dominate my life—and the lives of many of those around me—for much of the next six years.

Our commitment and perseverance paid off: we sued the federal government, and the Court of Appeals ruled unanimously in our favor. It was a stinging rebuke of the U.S. Department of Health and Human Services (the parent agency of CMS), which was forced to make reimbursement payments to groups of hospitals that had appealed the issue. The total of those payments represented one of the largest legal settlements ever by the Medicare program.

The story that follows has several elements. One is the lengths to which the federal government will go to block any claims against it and resist paying any damages—even after a federal court has ruled against it. Another element is how extraordinarily complicated it can be to take legal action against the federal government. We ultimately prevailed, but simply having the facts on our side was insufficient. We also had a group of people who worked together as a team and who were not afraid to be tenacious when the circumstances called for it. No less important, they had the capacity to argue amongst themselves without letting their disagreements become personal, and they continued to believe in each other even amid significant setbacks.

Finally, I had to shut out the naysayers who said we were highly unlikely to win and that I should worry about retaliation from the federal government for even pursuing the case. My mindset, which one of my attorneys characterized as "beyond fear," was fundamental to our success.

All these elements point to the indisputable fact that while the government can sometimes deliver solutions, it can also create problems. Big problems.

# ABOUT ME

I was born in Baltimore City in 1945 and, from the age of twelve, grew up in the city's Hamilton neighborhood. My father was the son of an immigrant from Greece; my mother was an American of German descent. My father worked twelve-hour days, six days a week, and never earned more than $10,000 a year. Until I was twelve, we lived in a row house, where I slept on a fold-up canvas cot in our living room (I was an only child), with the upstairs rented to tenants to make ends meet. We then moved to a modest single-family home, purchased for $10,000, in 1958. That was about the time we got our first phone; our first television had only come two years earlier. We did not have a car until I was seventeen, when we purchased a used Ford from a family friend for $200.

I attended public schools (other than Catholic school for the fifth through eighth grades) and walked the two-mile round-trip every day. In the summers, I worked for one of my high school teachers who also had a construction business building houses. I moved dirt, mixed concrete, and dug ditches—for twenty-five cents an hour. I also mowed lawns and raked leaves.

I was the first person from either side of my family to graduate from high school (my father completed tenth grade; my mother, sixth). After earning a diploma from Baltimore Polytechnic Institute, an all-boys public school at the time, I enrolled in Baltimore Junior College but flunked out; my discovery of girls was a leading contributor to my poor grades. I then enrolled in a two-year accounting school called Baltimore Institute, and after graduation I started working at an accounting firm. In the evening, I took classes at the Baltimore College of Commerce (the school rented classroom space from a local YMCA) and graduated with a Bachelor of Science Degree in Accounting.

Shortly after completing my course work at the end of August of 1969, I was drafted into the Army. I was sent to Fort Bragg, in North Carolina, and figured I was destined for Vietnam. I did not want to go, but I was willing to because I believed it was my duty as an American citizen. When I was being processed at Fort Bragg at 2 a.m., a first lieutenant noticed I had an accounting background and recommended me for the Finance Corps, which was responsible for the Army's financial operations, such as payroll and resource management. I was assigned there after basic training, which surprised me since the light weapons infantry was in dire need of help during the war. I was later transferred to Fort Eustis, near Williamsburg, Virginia, where I lived for about four months, and then reassigned to Fort Meade, not far from Baltimore. I was discharged in October 1970 due to my father's ill health. My one year of service gave me a much greater appreciation for what the military does and why it is needed.

A few months after my discharge, I started a job at Baltimore's St. Agnes Hospital, where I worked in finance and created an internal audit department. This marked the beginning of my career in healthcare. In 1975, I left St. Agnes for Baltimore

County General Hospital, where I worked as the controller until 1978. Having recently divorced from my first wife, it was here that I met the woman who would become my second wife, Jayne Koskinas. (As I will explain in more detail in Chapter 15, Jayne was a remarkable woman who had an important role in the appeal that is the subject of this book. I also document her battle with breast cancer and how that battle has helped influence my philanthropic activity since the appeal concluded.)

I later joined the Southern Maryland Medical Center as Chief Finance Officer, but soon discovered a number of questionable practices (such as charging patients for pillows) that I wanted no part of, so I departed after only six weeks. My departure created a challenge. Suddenly, I was unemployed with no obvious job prospects. But an acquaintance, Graham Atkinson, who would ultimately work with me on this appeal, was working as director of research at the State of Maryland's Health Services Cost Review Commission, which had been established in 1971 to promote cost containment, access to care, equity, financial stability, and hospital accountability. It also set rates for all payers, including Medicare and Medicaid. Graham asked if I would like a job there. He said it was temporary and would pay less than what I was making previously. I accepted and was glad I did, as the experience placed me at the nexus of healthcare and public policy. Much of what I learned there prepared me for jobs I would undertake in the future, such as the Healthcare Financial Management Association and Touche Ross, a large international accounting and consulting firm.

· · ·

At the Cost Review Commission, I learned a mathematical formula that would be critical to the knowledge I brought to the case against the federal government much later, known as the Laspeyres index (named for the German economist who devised it). One way it is used nowadays is to set payment rates, including Medicare's reimbursement rates. The index also lays the foundation for the budget neutrality (BN) calculation that was at the heart of our case against the federal government.

This calculation platform is used to measure or estimate current prices relative to those of a base period. A Laspeyres price index is computed by taking the ratio of the total cost of purchasing a specified group of commodities at current prices to the cost of that same group at base-period prices and multiplying by 100. The base-period index number is thus 100, and periods with higher price levels have index numbers greater than 100. And those below the base-period index number have an index of less than 100.

While it is less complicated than it sounds, it does take time and effort to fully understand how it should be applied when calculating and budget neutralizing Medicare reimbursement rates. Had I never learned about the index, and had I never understood how and when it needed to be modified when rate system attributes change, I never would have spotted CMS's error—and I never would have pursued the case that dominated my life for six years.

# CARS

When I was not immersing myself in the minutia of Medicare and hospital finance, I was pursuing my other passion: cars.

The first car I bought was a 1965 Chevy Chevelle, though I only had it for about a year before it was stolen. I replaced it with a Chevy Nova, and that is about the time I started drag racing at Capitol Raceway, in Crofton, Maryland. I loved the experience, and it gave me the urge to buy a sports car. I eventually settled on a beautiful 1971 sunflower yellow Corvette Stingray.

I continued racing, off and on, for many years, but it subsided after I married Jayne in 1984, and I sold the Corvette the following year. By 1991, I was ready to own another sports car, and I bought a Mitsubishi 3000 GT VR4. Driving it back from the dealership was a wake-up call: I wasn't as good a driver as I remembered, so I enrolled in a driving school offered by Sports Car Club of America, which also sponsors amateur racing. My training made it possible for me to begin road racing.

I entered some races with a 1972 BMW 2002 and set some track records. I later acquired a 1992 BMW 325, and eventually worked with someone I had met through racing circles, Ed York, to build a custom 325 together. I later started competing in the Grand American Road Racing Series and then moved on to the International Motor Sports Association, in which I have competed since 2006. A friend of Jayne's once asked her what she thought of my racing. She replied, "When men are having a midlife crisis, they can get into drugs, sex, or sports. It seems like sports is the least bad option."

In racing sports cars—endurance racing, specifically—it is exhilarating to drive 170 miles per hour or more, but there is a lot more to racing than pure speed. Other key factors include the skill of the driver (turns, for example, are the most challenging aspect of racing), the efficiency and expertise of the collective team (which does the rapid-fire maintenance and refueling during pit stops), and, increasingly, performance-related data, such as speed, throttle position, brake pressure, and steering angle.

My experience with racing helped shape how I approached my prolonged fight with the federal government—a theme I will explore in more detail later in the book. But underpinning the fight was my deep understanding of the Medicare hospital payment systems and related adjustments that were fundamental to the lawsuit I pursued on behalf of hundreds of hospitals.

## SUMMARY

- I grew up in very modest circumstances—my family did not have a phone in our home until I was twelve, and we did not own a car until I was seventeen.

- I have been working in and around the healthcare finance for forty years.

- For much of my adult life, when not immersing myself in the minutia of Medicare and hospital finance, I was pursuing my other passion: cars.

# 2

# THE MEDICARE INDUSTRIAL COMPLEX

The "Medicare Industrial Complex" shapes everything that happens with Medicare—which policies get implemented and which don't, which institutions win favor and which don't, and who gets hired and promoted and who doesn't. There is a lot at stake: total Medicare spending in 2018 was $750 billion.

The appeal that is the subject of this book was shaped by my understanding of the Medicare Industrial Complex, which I've worked in and around for decades. While I did not have the power to make the Medicare Industrial Complex do precisely what I wanted—no one has that power, not even the president and his appointees—my understanding of how it works was deep enough that I could increase the likelihood that our appeal would succeed. How much my overall understanding contributed to our eventual success would be impossible to quantify, but without it, I think it is almost certain our appeal would have failed.

# UNDERSTANDING MEDICARE

The Medicare program, which came into existence in 1965, was primarily created to provide acute, outpatient, and physician care for the elderly. In 1972, it was expanded to include care for the disabled and those with end-stage renal disease (ESRD). The Medicare program intersects with the Medicaid program, which primarily covers acute and outpatient care for the poor, but also covers the so-called "dual eligible," i.e., those eligible for Medicaid but entitled to Medicare, which covers long-term care.

• • •

Most federal programs are initially established for a specific patient population and a defined set of services. But, as with all federal programs, interest groups lobby or advocate for program expansion, frequently without any consideration for the longer-term implications. These advocacy efforts are usually based on analyses that are developed to prove a narrow point of view. Many advocacy groups turn into zealots, believing that any means to achieve their objective are justified, which often leads them to fabricate facts and analyses to support the desired end. The result is that these programs expand exponentially over time. The Medicare program has been no different.

There are several key players in the Medicare Industrial Complex.

Regulators: I have found that regulators are primarily career bureaucrats who ultimately desire power and they endure beyond political generations. Since a regulator is nothing without the power to regulate, many top regulators thrive on that power and even lust after it. They want to rise in seniority so they can control greater portions of the program. And they often develop the view that their perspective is the only one that is correct. This occurs without regard for whether they have worked in the industry they regulate or have the relevant understanding thereof. And the power of these regulators has been growing. As Congress has been less likely to reach agreement on the specific legislative provisions of the bills it passes related to Medicare (as well as other programs), the broad statutory language that gets approved gives regulators expanded authority and responsibility. This, coupled with court decisions that have served to give regulators more discretion, influence the policy development processes and who makes key decisions about how programs are administered and implemented.

Industry representatives: These players lobby Congress and the regulatory agencies. They are provider/trade associations, such as the American Hospital Association and the American Association of Retired Persons. These groups advocate on behalf of their members but often also advocate for the association itself. The main purpose of these associations or groups is to satisfy their members, not all of whom are equal because the dues being paid are based on their size. They are funded mainly by membership dues, so the associations often need to answer the question from their members of, "What have you done for me lately?" As a result, the leaders of these groups spend much of their time telling each member why the association is needed.

For-profit companies: These include provider companies (such as hospitals) but also the drug companies, insurers, device manufacturers, and service companies that provide services to the healthcare sector. They have a special interest—their own. For these individuals/entities, changes can be achieved to generate greater revenue for their organizations or as a strategic negative weapon against a competitor. As a result, policy changes are not necessarily straightforward, clear, or advantageous to program beneficiaries.

Special interest lobbyists: These include the providers that engage their own lobbying firms for a special purpose or have them in place of their associations. They are either large enough to have their own internal lobbying function or they hire an outside firm. They have their own, unique perspective and can part ways with their association on some or all issues.

Members of Congress: Congress is a caste system. Most of the clout is with those at the top of the hierarchy, but others can gain influence if they band together against the congressional leadership. But doing this can be very risky because the individual members will eventually need either votes or some sort of concession from the leadership. In dealing with their constituents, most politicians are good at saying "yes" but seem to be unable to say "no," even when they should. When politicians are running for re-election, it is often more important for them to show that they have *tried* to deliver for their constituents than to have actually done so.

# HOW PROGRAMS REALLY WORK

With any federal program, there are two basic pieces of the policy framework: the size of the pie and how it gets sliced. Interest groups lobby to get more people and services covered by the program—which means trying to increase the size of the pie. This is not to say that there is any rhyme or reason behind the expansion of service types. As programs grow, there is rarely, if ever, any focus on what services should be reduced or eliminated. This is the bane of all federal programs.

Whenever a federal program is created, all interest groups line up at the trough. As with any feeding pool, a frenzy sets in. (This is usually pie slicing.) The big "pigs" feed first, pushing the smaller pigs to the rear. Thus, the smallest pigs need to be more cunning or more vocal (because they lack the talent or patience) to argue for a seat at the table and access to the limited food supply. Therefore, rather than find alternative sources of food, it's always easier to advocate (often more loudly) that they be included in the program and therefore deserve a seat at the table.

Because of the dynamics of the pie sizing and slicing, all interested parties need to be constantly advocating for *something* in order to remain relevant. At some point, the size of the pie will stop growing and, in rare instances, will even contract. When this happens, the interest groups will engage in attempts to preserve their slice of the pie or work to expand their portion at the expense of others—in the trade, this is referred to as a "food fight." Accordingly, they are always playing either offense or defense. If they are not playing one or the other, they will lose.

One element of the federal government's response to COVID-19 helped illuminate how the Medicare Industrial Complex works. Washington authorized $175 billion to help hospitals, doctors' practices, and other healthcare providers cope with the costs associated with COVID-19. The formula used to distribute the first $30 billion showed how the system works.

Rather than allocating all the money (none of which needed to be repaid) to facilities that were overwhelmed with COVID-19 care, only $10 billion went to such facilities. The other $20 billion was allocated to healthcare providers entirely based on the level of their Medicare reimbursements in 2019. The number of COVID-19 patients they were treating was immaterial. North Carolina's Secretary of Health and Human Services spoke to *Newsweek* about the flaws in this approach:

> I think the current distribution will send most of the money to [. . .] the financially strong institutions with big pockets of money from commercial and Medicare payers, and the ones who are our safety net are really going to get hurt here. At the same time that we are trying to fight a crisis that is impacting our lower economic communities, we are not funding the providers who serve those communities.

While CMS modified how it allocated the next $20 billion, the episode showed the influence of the Medicare Industrial Complex. Even amid a national crisis, those with the most influence managed to secure funding for their operations based on vague criteria. While they might not have had an immediate need for the funding, they lined up to get it anyway.

The Medicare program is subjected to advocacy from hospitals, physicians (and the physician specialties), anesthetists, therapists, dietitians, and so on. Each of these groups advocates for expanded payments and coverage for populations of interest to them and their members. To make matters more complicated, there is inequality among the members of the trade associations representing these entities. Many, such as hospitals, levy membership fees, which are based on provider revenues. Therefore, larger hospitals pay more dues than smaller ones and, accordingly, are inherently more important to the association/organization. Many associations have attempted to create non-dues-based income streams, which are intended to counteract the clout of the larger dues-paying members. Some associations have succeeded with this, but most have not. As a result, the member bias is still prevalent in most of these organizations.

There is also a disparity across associations that is based on size. The California Hospital Association, for example, counts nearly five hundred hospitals as members. The Vermont Association of Hospitals and Health Systems, by comparison, has only sixteen members. Who do you think is more important to the American Hospital Association (and, perhaps, to Congress)?

Other advocacy groups also lobby the Medicare program. This includes organizations like the American Association of Retired Persons (AARP). One would think their interests are always aligned with Medicare's beneficiaries—in other words, their members—but not necessarily. The AARP has expanded its non-dues revenue, and this has transformed the organization. It now receives a percentage of the fees on many, if not all, the products it endorses and peddles to its members. These products include everything from auto insurance to the supplemental Medicare insurance. Because of these non-dues revenues, the AARP does not need to be as responsive to its membership and can focus more on the interests of the larger organization. And it does. In fact, the expanded coverage that was part of the Patient Protection and Affordable Care Act, which AARP supported, gave rise to products that the Association sold to its members. The AARP's support was striking, given that the PPACA included $500 billion in payment reductions to Medicare providers over its first ten years.

The intersection of the Medicare and Medicaid programs is also problematic. There is very little coordination between them, so they often work at cross-purposes—like the driver of a car simultaneously pressing down on both the accelerator and the brake. Problems also arise as a result of dual-eligible beneficiaries who have portions of their services covered by each program.

· · ·

The federal government is also under attack by the states, which lobby to shift more of their responsibility to the federal government. The feds have also attempted to shift costs to states, but the U.S. Senate limits this because it is inherently a state-sensitive body.

# HOW IT PLAYS OUT IN PRACTICE

The Medicare program has a larger concentrated pool of dollars than Medicaid. Medicare's growth rate is usually constrained or restricted. The pie is sliced through a series of adjustments that are applied to the base payment rate. For example, payments to the hospitals for a specific patient include a base payment rate, but there are other adjustments to the rate that impact how the pool of dollars is divided. Some adjustments are budget neutral (e.g., the wage adjustment), while others are not (e.g., the disproportionate share adjustment). Budget neutral adjustments do not change the size of the pie. But non-budget neutral payments can and often do. There are adjustments for area wage differences (e.g., New York City hospitals are paid a different adjusted rate than those in rural Vermont); case complexity (an open-heart surgery is much more costly than a cataract surgery); and dispro-portionate share (effectively an add-on to the rate to compensate for hospitals that have a large number of Medicaid patients whose pre-existing conditions increase the treatment costs at hospitals).

Thus, any hospital that has a specific interest in the payments that are the byproduct of the base rate, and/or any series of adjust-ments, lobbies for the adjustment to be performed in a particular manner and level. These lobbying battles involve many different categories of institutions: teaching and non-teaching hospitals; urban and rural hospitals; hospitals with significant numbers of Medicaid patients, and those with very few; hospitals with very complex caseloads, and those whose cases are far simpler.

Therefore, the Medicare program has expanded because, in many instances, congressional pressure makes it easier to say "yes" than "no" to those who are advocating for their interests. Accordingly, many of Medicare's polices are uncoordinated and often function at cross-purposes, to say nothing of the interven-tion of misinformed regulators. (There is also the unfortunate phenomenon of regulators believing that their knowledge is supe-rior to everyone else's.) This lack of coordination and occasional conflict are outgrowths of policies evolving for what are often narrow, parochial reasons that were never part of any grand long-term strategy, but merely designed to get money where insiders wanted it to go.

# PROTECTIONISM

There is a well-documented tendency for companies/organizations to gradually begin acting in their self-interest (or in the case of for-profit entities, the interests of its senior executives), as opposed to supporting those the company/organization is intended to serve, such as stockholders or patients. The same happens to the associations that advocate for payment level adjustments. Similarly, states will often advocate for their respective interests, rather than for what is best for the program or program beneficiaries. This diversion of interest occurs in a subtle way, over time, and it can be almost imperceptible to the public and the members of the association.

Medicare, like the rest of government, is not insulated from governmental bureaucracies that evolve over time. The increased complexity of the Medicare payment system breeds an expansion of bureaucracy and greater segmentation of duties and responsibilities. The program staff become more segregated in the components of the systems they manage. Many of those who work in the agency that administers Medicare do not understand or appreciate the full scope of how the elements of the payment system fit together, nor what the system is supposed to accomplish. But because the lobbyists often have a *better* understanding, they can target idiosyncratic surgical adjustments.

# REGULATORY CAPTURE

A related concept is referred to as "regulatory capture." This refers to situations in which the regulatory body begins to reflect the interests of the entities it is regulating. It can also refer to the regulated entities having excessive influence over the regulators. Another scenario, which also involves career-minded regulators, is that they accumulate too much power and become resentful of any efforts to curtail it, even if those efforts are directed by political appointees who are senior to them. Thus, bureaucrats often do whatever they like. They know they will remain at the regulatory agency long after political appointees and administrations leave office—often *decades* longer—and that it can be exceedingly difficult to dislodge them. They are firmly and inextricably entrenched.

## SUMMARY

- The Medicare Industrial Complex shapes everything that happens with Medicare, but particularly policy, personnel, and the success or failure of the many different entities that advocate for expanded payments and coverage.

- Many Medicare polices are uncoordinated and operate at cross-purposes—a byproduct of the far-reaching advocacy efforts that are often narrow and parochial and ultimately dictate how large segments of the program's dollars are distributed.

- The increased complexity of the Medicare payment system breeds an expansion of bureaucracy and greater segmentation of duties and responsibilities.

# 3

# UNDERSTANDING BUDGET NEUTRALITY

T he core issue at stake in our lawsuit—budget neutrality (BN)—requires some explanation of precisely why it matters. To get to a more complete understanding, it's useful to know some of the history related to Medicare.

On July 30, 1965, President Lyndon Johnson traveled to the Truman Library in Independence, Missouri, to sign a landmark bill into law. The legislation created a federally funded program (Medicare) to provide healthcare to Americans aged sixty-five and above. President Johnson had traveled to Independence in recognition of President Harry Truman who proposed a national health insurance fund, administered by the federal government, early in his presidency.

With the new law, said Johnson, "every citizen will be able, in his productive years when he is earning, to insure himself against the ravages of illness in his old age." He went on to lay out an even more expansive vision for what would be possible because of Medicare:

*No longer will older Americans be denied the healing miracle of modern medicine. No longer will illness crush and destroy the savings that they have so carefully put away over a lifetime so that they might enjoy dignity in their later years. No longer will young families see their own incomes, and their own hopes, eaten away simply because they are carrying out their deep moral obligations to their parents, and to their uncles, and their aunts. And no longer will this Nation refuse the hand of justice to those who have given a lifetime of service and wisdom and labor to the progress of this progressive country.*

The original payment system underpinning Medicare called for hospitals to be reimbursed based on the "reasonable costs" associated with serving Medicare patients. This system was essentially based on the number of days a patient was in the hospital, and so the longer the length of a patient's stay, the more the hospital received in reimbursement. Predictably, lengths of stay soared.

To address the increasing costs per stay, the system was changed with the enactment of Tax Equity and Fiscal Responsibility Act of 1982 (TEFRA). This system was still cost-based, but with a per-discharge limit on the amount any hospital would be paid for each discharged patient. The so-called "target rate" (the limit) per discharge was based on each hospital's own costs per discharge. For the sake of simplicity, let's say the limit was $1,000. If a hospital's cost was $900, it would receive an extra payment for a portion of the difference of the $100 (reflecting the difference between the cost and the limit). But if the hospital's cost was $1,200, it would be penalized, having a portion of the extra $200 taken back.

Since the TEFRA limit was based on hospital-specific costs, there were limited adjustments. Accordingly, hospitals that were inefficient when their target rate was established could garner an incentive payment by having its costs come in below their target rate. Conversely, hospitals that had an efficient or lean target base had difficulty in making things work under TEFRA. This created the wrong incentives for hospitals.

Not surprisingly, Congress modified that system in 1983, and ordered the Secretary of Health and Human Services (HHS) to create a system whereby hospitals would receive fixed payments for specific patient services—a prospective rate system—known as the Inpatient Prospective Payment System (IPPS). This system gave the HHS Secretary the authority to determine what would be a "reasonable payment" for such services. Though with hospitals incentivized to spend more (and be reimbursed more)—if the cost incurred was less than the base payment, they could pocket the difference—there were legitimate concerns about the failure to control costs. Upon initiation, the IPPS system had 383 distinct rates (calculated using a set of weights that were budget neutral) in addition to the other IPPS adjustments.

The IPPS system was based upon a standardized payment rate per discharge that would initially be the same for all hospitals. The rate would have some required adjustments—for area wage differences, for the complexity of the case, for the teaching status of the hospital, and for serving a disproportionate share of low-income patients. Because the standardized payment rate was developed in advance of the year it was to take effect, it provided some level of predictability for hospitals and the government.

Congress modified the payment system in the 1997 Balanced Budget Act (BBA) to further restrain cost per discharge. One of the BBA provisions established a "rural floor" (RF) under which no urban hospital would be paid less than what the rural hospitals in that state were paid. The issue surrounding the RF adjustment is the subject of much of the remainder of this story.

It's important to understand that the calculation of prospective IPPS payment rates is based on an estimated average cost incurred by hospitals for each patient who is treated and discharged. This figure is known as the "standardized amount." Another part of the prospective payment rates is the area wage index (AWI), which measures variations in hourly wages found across different geographic areas and applies those differences to the Medicare reimbursement formula. Since 1994, the AWI has been updated annually.

Critical to our case was that the standardized amount is not subject to a complete "reset" each year. Instead, a base year is used, and the amount is recalculated according to annual inflation and other measures.

The concept of budget neutrality (BN) is applied to select portions of the Medicare payment system. The BN concept is generally required to be applied by the relevant statute. Consider the sum total of all Medicare payments as a pie, and for the sake of simplicity we'll say that there are payments going to ten different patients, each of which is represented by a slice of pie. BN means that if one of those patients is going to be getting a larger slice of pie, the Medicare administrators need to figure how to reapportion the remaining slices since the pie cannot expand.*

........................................................................................

\* It's important to understand that while Medicare was originally supposed to be a fund that would steadily accumulate capital; that's not how it functions today. Instead, money paid in is immediately paid out for current services or borrowed to fund the rest of the government. As a result, there is no cash accumulation, in effect making it a transfer fund.

The IPPS system is composed of a rate per patient discharge, calculated using a series of adjustments. BN is applied to applicable adjustments (that are specified in statute), which are used in developing the IPPS.

The Medicare program can select one of two methods when applying BN: the cumulative method and the non-cumulative method. Under the cumulative method, the BN adjustment for any particular year for an applicable adjustment is applied to the payment rate and, therefore, adjusts the rate in perpetuity (up or down). Under the non-cumulative method, the BN adjustment is applied for each particular year (having reversed the effect of the prior year's adjustment) and the adjustment is recalculated each year anew.

In our situation, the BN grew out of a provision of the Balanced Budget Act. The goal was to foster greater funding parity between rural and urban hospitals in the same state. To that end, the provision set state-by-state minimums, or "floors," for the payments (achieved through the relative AWIs that are used to calculate federal reimbursement rates, which in turn are used to pay all Medicare hospitals). And henceforth, these payment floors for urban hospitals could be no less than the payments for rural hospitals, nor could the adjustment change the value of all the reimbursements in total.

This latter provision was the requirement for BN called for by Congress. The Secretary of Health and Human Services elected to interpret this requirement by adjusting the standardized amount for the relative wage differences. (Despite the fact that the adjustment is referred to as the "rural" floor, this policy is applied to and benefits qualifying "urban" hospitals.)

The implications of this were significant, as the Court of Appeals later explained in its ruling on our case:

*Potentially, the rural floor could affect the total amount of money Medicare pays hospitals each year. For example, if CMS increased the wage indexes of urban hospitals to bring them in line with the wage indexes of rural hospitals in the same state, payments to those urban hospitals would increase. All other things being equal, the aggregate amount of Medicare payments would increase as well. But Congress required the Secretary to take steps to ensure that all other things would not be equal. It mandated that the rural floor be "budget neutral." In other words, it required the Secretary to implement the rural floor in a manner that would have no effect on the annual total of Medicare payments made to all hospitals throughout the country for inpatient services.*

Understanding the essence of BN was fundamental to our case, because the governing statute requires that changes to select portions of the formula can't affect the total of the aggregate payments. (An illustration of how BN works is in Appendix 2.) Our argument regarding the RF rested on our conviction that CMS had made a mistake when applying a formula to reimburse certain hospitals, a mistake that was baked into the formula and repeated every year. That meant that because the error was integral to the "standardized rate" used as a basis to pay all of the hospitals, all hospitals were being underpaid each year, and BN was not being achieved (thus violating a clear directive from Congress). And with the errors being carried over from year to year, they compounded, growing larger every year.

I have shared this history not only because it provides the underpinning for our case but also because it helps convey the complexity of the issues involved. A comprehensive understanding of budget neutrality depended on also understanding how it was affected by the area wage index, standardized amounts, and the IPPS. I was likely not the only person who understood how all these pieces fit together. But I was (apparently) the only one who identified the error and, was curious enough to ask the question that led to CMS (unknowingly) acknowledging the formula error, and had the determination and courage to sue them for making the error.

## SUMMARY

- The core issue at stake in our lawsuit was a measure known as "budget neutrality," as applied to a provision called the "rural floor" (RF), which was designed to foster greater funding parity between rural and urban hospitals in the same state.

- Under BN, there is a defined pool of funds. Any increase in payments attributable to a change in one area wage adjustment must be offset by a corresponding reduction in all other area wage adjustments (and therefore payments).

- In our lawsuit, we were alleging that the federal government had made an error in calculating BN, and that the error was duplicating and had been baked into the formula, which meant hospitals had been underpaid for several years. This underpayment meant that the federal government did not satisfy the statutorily mandated BN—in other words, the government violated the law.

# 4

# SEEKING GUIDANCE FROM THE GOVERNMENT

I sent the original email to CMS because I wanted to confirm the data elements the agency used in their formula to achieve BN. In the technical response, the CMS rep repeatedly referenced the use of "wage data" as part of the BN calculation.

This told me that the administrators of the Medicare program were making an error in how they calculated budget neutrality. They were relying on area wage data, indicating that they were recalculating the AWI each year, which is based on hospital wage levels in different geographic areas. The administrators should have been using the relative AWIs that had been applied in the prior and current rate years. To the untrained eye, the change would have seemed insignificant. But there were far-reaching implications.

"Holy crap," I said to myself, after receiving the reply from CMS. "They're computing this incorrectly." To corroborate my thinking, I forwarded the CMS email to Graham Atkinson for his review. As I mentioned earlier, Graham and I had worked together for three decades and we had both been part of the Maryland hospital rate-setting commission. Through this work, I knew that Graham understood the Laspeyres index (more on that below) and would be able to judge whether CMS had applied it incorrectly. Graham called me and confirmed that the calculation was in error.

# GRAHAM ATKINSON

I have been operating in and around the world of hospital finance for most of my professional life. As a result, I suspect I know more about the subject than 99.9 percent of the population. But I would put Graham Atkinson within that one-tenth of one percent, though he brought a different perspective.

Graham is a textbook example of a math nerd (he wouldn't dispute the characterization). He has a doctorate in math from Oxford. He attends a math camp for adults almost every year, and his interests include Mayan hieroglyphics (the Mayans developed a highly sophistical mathematical system). He's also thrifty (perhaps a function of his Scottish heritage) and he can be socially awkward. I've told him that the definition of a mathematician is someone who lacks the interpersonal skills to become an actuary.

All joking aside, Graham, while functioning in cameo roles, was a critical member of our team throughout the appeal and settlement process. I could throw virtually any question at him and get a thoughtful answer—as long as it involved numbers.

Graham and I met in 1978, when we were colleagues at the Maryland Health Services Cost Review Commission (the regulatory agency that regulated Maryland's hospital rates). It was during this time that I began to understand, thanks in part to Graham, the Laspeyres index—a formula used in price statistics that would become a critical part of identifying the Medicare error at the heart of our appeal. We became good friends and through the years we worked together in different capacities.

Graham was an integral part of the appeal. His principal role was to ensure that we were properly focused on the methodology and explaining it correctly, having simplified it for the courts. He participated in many of the most important meetings involving the attorneys. He was also willing to challenge me on my positions—not in a hostile way, but to make sure I had considered a range of options.

During the settlement process, Graham also helped develop two methodologies for calculating the amounts due the hospitals. This was a labor-intensive process, as we went through twenty iterations with DataGen (another partner in this appeal) to get the calculation right.

I had total confidence in Graham's ability to work through complicated issues and give me airtight answers. I was extremely fortunate to have him as part of the team.

What CMS officials didn't realize prior to my follow-up email, was that as a consequence of not using the relative fiscal year AWIs (when combined with CMS's use of the cumulative BN method), and instead recalculating the impact using the wage *data*, they were using the incorrect data variable. Their use of the word "data" told me that they were not using the AWIs for each of the two years involved. And that meant they were violating the RF-BN provision of the Balanced Budget Act, which called for funding parity between rural and urban hospitals in the same state.

After thinking through all the scenarios CMS could be using, and concluding that they were duplicating the adjustment, I wanted confirmation. Following a discussion with Graham, I wrote back to Nina a few hours later with a follow-up question that hinted at an error in CMS's methodology.

*Thanks, your response was to the point. I have one very focused question that deals with the rural floors.*

*If there is an area that becomes subject to the floor in year 1 when we do the BN using the without floor AWI and with floor AWI, this differential is built into the standardized rate (in my hypothetical the rate would appropriately be reduced). The following year when we do the BN we would use the without floor AWI and the with floor AWI in defining BN. Recognizing that the relative AWIs may have changed, why doesn't this duplicate in some respect the carve out for the application of the floor. This would seem to occur unless we used the old floor in the base and the new floor for the estimates in the new period. Am I missing something? Thanks. T*

I'll never know what Nina and her colleagues thought when they read the follow-up email, but I've imagined that it was something akin to, "Oh shit."

I thought then, and think today, that CMS had made an honest mistake at some point after the 1997 passage of the Balanced Budget Act (probably in the second year), and this mistake simply became embedded into the agency's BN calculation formula over time.

While seemingly a small error at the outset, the implications of this improper implementation were quite significant because of the compounding effect of the error. We had initially estimated that this mistake had cost the hospitals in question about 0.5 percent annually, but we were unsure of when the error actually began. It would be another six years before CMS corrected its mistake, and it only did so when provoked by the court's decision.

Some might wonder why no hospital officials had ever uncovered this mistake. The simple answer is that CMS said it was using a cumulative approach but not disclosing its calculations; therefore, there was no way of knowing that errors had crept into the system. Prior to this, the hospital industry had never performed a large-scale test to ascertain if BN was being correctly calculated, nor did they ask questions about BN. The industry just assumed that CMS was correct. *Had I not sent my email to CMS, it's entirely possible the errors never would have been uncovered.*

Rather than cooperating with me, CMS officials with whom I had been exchanging emails stopped responding to my inquiries. They went into radio silence and then in court went to extraordinarily lengths to try to deny ever having seen my inquiries. (Their efforts were later ridiculed by a federal judge involved with our lawsuit against CMS, as I document later.)

About a month after the initial exchange of emails, I submitted a comment letter to CMS, which was based on the email exchange. But I did not specifically reference the exchange, nor did I include the email in the letter, because at this juncture we did not want to alert others in the industry to the discrepancy we had uncovered. But I did make clear that the BN calculation was erroneous, as the following passage shows:

*Based on information recently provided to us by* [CMS] *staff, we have learned that each year* [CMS] *uses payment vari-*

*ables (including the* [rural-floor-adjusted wage indexes]*) for the rural floor* [budget-neutrality] *adjustment that measure the total annual estimated effect of the application of the rural floor, not the incremental year-to-year change of the rural floor impact. This would be appropriate if, in applying the current year's rural floor* [budget-neutrality] *adjustment,* [CMS] *backed out of the calculation the prior year's rural floor* [budget-neutrality] *adjustment.* [CMS] *does not do this, however, and instead permanently locks in the rural floor* [budget-neutrality] *adjustment into the standardized amount. As a result, most of the rural floor* [budget-neutrality] *adjustment is improperly duplicated each year, with compounding effect.*

Lest there be any confusion, I also specified what was at stake: "This duplication over-adjusts the standardized amount for the effect of the rural floor, and has the effect of improperly lowering payments to all hospitals through a [budget-neutrality] adjustment that is too large."

## SUMMARY

- The error in calculating BN was a byproduct of Medicare administrators using an incorrect data variable.

- Had I not emailed someone at Medicare to ask how BN was calculated, it's entirely possible that the error never would have been uncovered.

# 5

# THE GOVERNMENT GOES MUM . . . SO I START RECRUITING LAWYERS, HOSPITALS, AND A FINANCIER

The silence from CMS convinced me that the only way to get it to fix this error would be through a court order. But I also knew that suing a federal agency would be a very long process—at least three years—and a very expensive undertaking. Furthermore, even if we took the case to court, I knew that the odds were against us. It's not easy to win a case against the federal government, and it's even more challenging when you're dealing with an issue as complex as this one, since courts have given government agencies "deference" in complex matters. I knew that if our case could be crystallized as a legal dispute, we would have a much better chance of winning.

If we were going to have any hope of winning, we were going

to need a comprehensive strategy, and it would have to start with recruiting in two essential areas: lawyers and hospitals. We were going to need first-rate lawyers who understood the complexities of Medicare reimbursement issues, as well as the underlying mathematics, and could explain all of this to a judge. And we were going to need hospitals that had been adversely affected by the CMS error to appeal the issue and join our case. Virtually all hospitals nationally had been affected by the error because it was in the base payment rate.

In the summer of 2006, I retained a Baltimore-based firm to help me with the comment letter. Three attorneys were involved, all of whom I had worked with previously. As I noted earlier, we were extremely careful in drafting the letter, as we did not want to tip off others about the email exchange that we considered to be the proverbial smoking gun. We all were comfortable with how the letter turned out, and it accomplished precisely what was needed at that early stage.

The next step was recruiting hospitals to join the appeal, and that process began in the fall of 2006. I contacted several of my current clients, explained the issue, and asked if they would be willing to sign on and pay an upfront fee of $5,000, $7,500, or $10,000. The response was generally along the lines of, "Well, yeah, we'd do it because it's you." My reaction was, "What if it wasn't me and you didn't know me?" We initially envisioned that between 100 and 125 hospitals would sign on, and the vast majority of them would not know me. The early responses told me that folks who would be target candidates would need some coaxing to join the appeal.

In the pitch to my hospital clients, we walked them through the issue in general terms—few of them had ever considered how

BN was calculated—and we told them there was a significant amount of money at stake (see Appendix 4 for an example of the letter we sent to hospitals). We could not disclose entirely what the issue was about, however, and most hospitals didn't understand or know of the issue at the time. Alas, they were generally ambivalent, which surprised me, given that these clients were familiar with my work and they stood to make significant gains if CMS changed the formula. I nonetheless started approaching other healthcare consulting firms to see if they would be interested in having their hospital clients get involved.

I knew there were many hospitals in New York and that most of them had high Medicare payments, which meant they would be affected more significantly by the CMS error. One of my prior associates at Touche Ross from the late 1980s was based in New York. I figured he had a lot of hospital contacts in the state, first because they were previous clients, and second because he was previously CEO of a New York-based health system.

I called him, explained the deal, and asked him to contact and market to the hospitals he knew. The deal with the hospitals would be an upfront fee of $10,000, plus a 25 percent contingency fee of whatever the hospital received from the appeal proceeds. (In other words, he would get a portion of whatever my firm recovered from the contingency fee. The fixed fee was to assure that my firm received some proceeds from the appeal to compensate for our efforts.) He said, "Let me think about it," and he promised to call me back. Two days later, he called and said, "Ted, I have Ron here with me. Can I put you on speaker?" I responded, "Yes."

Ron (not his real name) would not normally be part of any conversation, but right away I realized his role. I had known Ron previously and had done some work with his firm. Ron had built the firm over thirty years—its focus was reviewing hospital bills, mostly for union health and welfare funds and some other insurance companies. Importantly, Ron had just sold his firm for $1.2 billion.

My former associate said that he was thinking about our conversation two days earlier and mentioned it to Ron. Then Ron took over the conversation, which went something like this:

*Ron: Our mutual acquaintance was explaining to me that you found an error in Medicare payments and that it could be the basis for an appeal/lawsuit.*
*Ted: That's correct.*
*Ron: He said that you were concerned that hospitals might resist signing up if they had to pay an upfront fee.*
*Ted: Correct.*
*Ron: How many hospitals do you think would sign up if they did not have to pay an upfront fee?*
*Ted: A hell of a lot more than if they had to pay one.*
*Ron: What if someone would put up money to cover the legal fees? Would you give them a cut of the contingency fee?*
*Ted: Yes.*
*Ron: When do you think you could come up here and talk about it?*
*Ted: How about tomorrow?*
*Ron: Fine.*
*Ted: I'll call you back in 30 minutes and tell you when I'll be there.*

We met the next morning for two hours and worked out the

framework of a deal for Ron to fund the initial litigation. We had access to $1.2 million. With this funding in place, I changed the deal with potential hospitals to a 100 percent risk-based contingent fee of 25 percent of their yield from the appeal, plus $10,000 per hospital—both payable only if we won. Ron's role was akin to that of a venture capitalist. He was investing in me, with the idea that our case might result in a sizable payout by the federal government—a portion of which would go to him if we won the case.

Later joining our effort was an acquaintance of mine, who had been general counsel a New York-based health care company and who was then the managing partner in a large New York law firm. Together we approached the Hospital Association of New York State (HANYS) and met with several of their top administrative and policy folks. Mark Callan was their central policy guy, and once we explained the issue and showed him the email, he immediately understood it. We then developed an arrangement whereby HANYS would receive a percentage of the proceeds for the hospitals they brought into the appeal.

HANYS has a for-profit subsidiary, DataGen, which provides services to about half of the other state hospital associations. Agreements were developed with HANYS for the hospitals in New York state and with the subsidiary for the non-New York hospitals. We used DataGen to work with us during the appeal in performing modeling and other related appeal calculations. As part of our initial discussions, we had them sign a non-disclosure agreement, which enabled us to share the details of what we had uncovered, and what we thought they meant, but prevented the organizations from pursuing the matter on their own if they opted not to join our effort.

We then conducted a series of solicitation conference calls

with hospitals in New York and throughout the country. During the calls, Callan, Chris Keough (an attorney who would play a vital role in the case), and myself presented the facts and responded to questions. We had developed a standard contract letter of agreement for each hospital to sign, and while some hospitals/systems wanted a different letter, we held firm and did not change the terms. Most New York hospitals signed up.

By this time, our fear of a pile-on was in full swing. The head of an Indiana-based healthcare consulting firm was also marketing the issue to hospital associations—but at a lower fee. Unfortunately, he was handicapped by not having a clear understanding of the issue. He did work with the HANYS subsidiary on other issues, but steered clear of marketing the case in New York after the state association told him that if he went against their wishes, they would not work with him on other matters anywhere in the country and would tell other state associations to cut him off.

Our firm previously had the Texas Hospitals Association (THA) as a client, so we developed an agreement with them for the Texas hospitals, and since THA had a relationship with the Oklahoma Hospital Association, we solicited their hospitals also. We also contacted several other consulting firms and developed similar relationships. In the end, there were essentially two types of client hospitals: individual hospitals and hospitals that were a part of a commonly controlled system.

Many hospitals were supportive because we were potentially going to secure a significant amount of money for them, and they were not going to be charged anything unless we won. But we also encountered considerable skepticism. A large number of the hospitals we approached thought we couldn't win. Some were wary of challenging CMS. And one hospital CEO—someone I had known for years—insisted on knowing where the money was coming from to fund the legal effort. I couldn't tell him, since that was part of the deal with Ron, so he refused to be a party to the case. To my knowledge, he has never filed or been paid on this issue.

## SUMMARY

- Our ability to move forward depended on having a few people who could help identify hospitals to join our appeal and securing capital to fund our efforts. Our ability to attract both, with relative ease, was an encouraging sign.

# 6

# THE LEGAL EAGLES

P rior to mounting this legal effort, I had worked with a wide variety of lawyers over a twenty-year period. But I never could have predicted how much drama would be involved with the team of lawyers who were involved with this case.

After I decided to file an appeal, I approached the Baltimore-based law firm that had developed the initial comment letter. But because of the agreement with Ron, I wanted them to agree to a fee cap, which they wouldn't do. So I began looking around for another team that could represent us within our budget. I talked to several other law firms, including Vinson & Elkins, a large Houston-based firm, with a big practice in Washington, D.C., as I had an acquaintance there named Dennis Barry. They requested that I meet with a technical expert named Alan Dobson, who had once worked at CMS. After he signed a non-disclosure agreement, I explained the details of what I was pursuing. I shared the email with Dobson, and he immediately understood CMS's error.

# CHRISTOPHER KEOUGH

I first met Chris in the summer of 2006. I had discovered the duplicating error but could not come to terms with other firms on litigating the case. I contacted Vinson & Elkins and eventually met Chris late one afternoon, along with Dobson. The meeting lasted four hours. Toward the end of the meeting, Chris pulled out a clean sheet of paper and said, "Let me explain to you what I think the error is." He made a simple illustration that captured the essence of the issue. "Is this what the case is about?" he asked. When I said it was, he replied, "I can explain this to a judge." And that was the start of a close and valued relationship.

Chris would emerge as the architect of our long-term legal strategy, becoming both a trusted confidant to me, as well as a good friend. He is a very focused and intense individual. We got along very well. He is aggressive and has a very good understanding of the law and litigation strategy. He is one of the top attorneys I have ever worked with on Medicare law and regulation.

Chris principally served as a strategist for the litigation, shepherding the appeal processes at the administrative level and generally overseeing the litigation. He also had a prime role in drafting the settlement agreement, as well as negotiating the settlement framework and the settlement terms. He was instrumental in the development of all the briefs filed in the case.

While Chris had argued many cases at the D.C. Court of Appeals, one of his key contributions was having the foresight to get Paul Clement, a former U.S. Solicitor General, to argue the appeal. It was unselfish insights like these that led to our victory.

I came to terms with Vinson & Elkins, and they agreed to an $800,000 fee cap (they were the only credible firm I talked to that would agree to a fee cap). I was very happy with how my relationship with them developed. But given that approximately 730 hospitals subsequently elected to join our appeal (six times as many as we expected), we blew through the fee cap in about seven months. Recognizing that we were still in the early administrative filing stages of this issue, involving the initial year, and hadn't even gotten to court, we needed to have another fee discussion with the firm's management. They made clear they wanted to continue working with me, but they also wanted to be compensated accordingly.

That meant I had to go back to Ron, our funder. I explained the issues at the stake, and the potential for him to see a big payoff. He wanted my assurance that I was prepared to see the case through to the end if the fee structure was modified. When I said I would, he agreed to adjust their fee arrangement. Going forward, his percentage was applied after certain fees were treated as costs in determining the applicable percentage of the fees due. If the fee arrangement had not been adjusted, it would have had the effect of me paying for all the increased legal fees from my portion of these settlements—essentially eliminating my motivation. Ron astutely realized this.

# THE HOSPITAL ENGAGEMENT AGREEMENT

I worked with my former associate to draft the engagement agreement that was sent to the hospitals we were targeting for the appeal (a generic version of the agreement is contained in Appendix 4). The proposal spelled out for the hospitals the terms of the engagement we were proposing. It included a performance fee and a fixed fee per hospital. Both of these were payable only if the appeal was successful or if I was successful in reaching a settlement with the federal government (a settlement or resolution did not necessarily mean success in courts, so the door was open to a negotiated settlement, which often occurs).

As I mentioned earlier, the performance fee called for the hospitals to pay 25 percent of whatever funds were recovered following a successful appeal or settlement. The fixed fee, which was $10,000 per hospital, was dedicated to recovering the costs of pursuing the appeal.

Another key element of the agreement gave me the sole discretion to resolve or settle the issue for any and all appealed years. The agreement also specified that because I had arranged for the capital to fund the appeal, I retained the sole discretion to choose whether to terminate the appeal efforts. This decision could be based in part on the advice of counsel, but the agreement said that agreement from counsel was not required.

Ron liked that the ultimate authority rested with me and me alone, though that did not stop him from occasionally pushing me on certain matters, as I describe later. He was placing a bet on my ability to see the whole matter through, though we also agreed that if I couldn't proceed for any reason, such as illness or sudden incapacitation, then my associate, Graham Atkinson, would be in charge.

About two years into the engagement, my relationship with Vinson & Elkins changed. While the firm had one of the most

respected energy practices in the world, its senior partners concluded they didn't want to focus on their healthcare practice.
Many of the firm's healthcare partners, led by Dennis Barry, bro-
kered a deal for most of the healthcare-focused lawyers, including
all of the attorneys working on the appeal, to be merged into a
large Atlanta-based firm, King & Spalding. There was only one
attorney on our team, John Faust, who remained at Vinson &
Elkins and continued to work with us until the end of the appeal.

This change proved quite disruptive for me and our firm; it
was traumatic. I viewed the situation being akin to a doctor in
the middle of a surgery announcing he is leaving and passing the
reins to someone else. We had to go through a round of negotiations with the King & Spalding management committee, which at
times was quite complicated (something I expected). Because we
had exceeded the fee cap, we wanted to go forward on the basis
of a risk-based agreement. This meant that the partners/manage-
ment of both King & Spalding and Vinson & Elkins would need
to accept that they might not see any payoff if we lost the case.
And there would be no revenue or cash flow from this matter,
which meant that the firm(s) had to internally agree to fund the
compensation of those attorneys representing us, and to do so
for the duration of the proceedings, which was likely to be a few
years. Getting firms to agree to terms like these isn't easy, and we
were worried that King & Spalding would want to drop the case.

Fortunately, they were amenable to what we proposed, so we
followed our attorneys to their new firm. One attorney who later
joined King & Spalding, Stephanie Webster, emerged with Chris
as a key member of our legal team (she and Chris had also been
colleagues at another firm). Stephanie had previously worked in
the general counsel's office at CMS, and in addition to being a

great lawyer, her highly nuanced understanding of the agency greatly informed our strategy.

# STEPHANIE WEBSTER

Steph Webster was one of the critical players through the appeal and settlement process. She had worked at a few different firms, but of particular value was her experience in the general counsel's office at the Centers for Medicare and Medicaid Services. Chris had squared off against her in another case and was very impressed by her. Therefore, when the opportunity presented itself, he recruited her.

Steph joined our litigation team in late 2007. Her initial role was one of oversight connected to the appeal filing. But it quickly became apparent that she had litigation strategy insights and skills that would serve us well. Her approach is more subtle than Chris's style, which is more overt. In discussions or negotiations with Steph, you come away thinking, "That wasn't so bad." But after a few days you think, "Hey, she rolled us on that." That's a tribute to Steph's very subtle style.

Steph also added the women's perspective that is needed in any project; litigation is no different.

I knew we would be more likely to win if we had a variety of styles, perspectives, and insights. Steph was able provide insights on the government's perspective, given her CMS experience, as well as insights on how best to think the way to opposition thinks.

She also played a critical role in developing our briefs and in oral argument at the Court of Appeals. Along with Chris, she was a prime driver in winning the case.

Another King & Spalding attorney who would play a critical role for us was Paul Clement. Paul had been the solicitor general of the United States from June 2005 until June 2008—a role that had him argue cases before the U.S. Supreme Court on behalf of the federal government. He argued our case before the Court of Appeals, despite coming into the process after we had lost at the District Court. As I will explain later, he could not have argued the case any better.

Adding to the drama in October 2010, Steph and Chris concluded that King & Spalding was not a good fit for them and moved to the Washington office of Akin Gump, another powerhouse law firm. This entailed another round of negotiations with us and with the firms. Fortunately, Chris had made his move to Akin Gump contingent upon being able to continue to represent us, so the negotiation was smoother than the earlier one. Nonetheless, it meant that, at one point, my legal team consisted of an attorney from Vinson & Elkins (John Faust), two from King & Spalding (Paul Clement and Dennis Barry), and two from Akin Gump (Steph and Chris). Our formal agreement was with King & Spalding, with total fees to them split among the firms on an agreed-upon basis. As you might imagine, it was extremely complicated, given that multiple firms were now involved.

When Chris went to Akin Gump, one of the firm's partners was serving as the head of the Washington office for the California-based firm involved with RF BN appeal. As part of his move to Akin Gump, the firm agreed that this individual would need to terminate his relationship with the California-based firm. In the end, that firm opened its own D.C. office, so the attorney never needed to resign. Nevertheless, Chris took the right steps and Akin Gump was prepared to do the ethical thing, avoiding any conflict of interest.

# SUMMARY

- I knew that recruiting a talented team of lawyers would greatly increase my odds of defeating the federal government.

- Identifying the lawyers was relatively easy, but dealing with their law firms was quite difficult. However, we managed to strike agreements with them that enabled our work to proceed.

# 7

# DEVELOPING A LEGAL STRATEGY

A bove and beyond the recruitment of first-rate attorneys, there were two other key elements to our legal strategy. One element was how we wanted our case to move through the administrative appeals process and the other was the legal system. This is more complicated than it sounds.

The first step for any individual or institution challenging a determination reached by CMS is to file an appeal with the Provider Reimbursement Review Board (PRRB), which is an independent administrative panel within CMS that hears provider payment claims. We had no choice but to start with PRRB, but we believed that we needed to go to court to get a fair hearing, since PRRB, while technically independent, is often biased in favor of the status quo. That's because they don't have the authority to rule on issues that involve a challenge to a CMS statute and are bound by Medicare regulations and policies, whereas providers are only bound by the statute. Since we were challenging CMS on whether budget neutrality (a statutory requirement) applied here, our filing with PRRB argued that it lacked the appropriate authority to rule on our case, and that the matter should be granted expedited judicial review. The PRRB agreed. And we filed suit in federal District Court.

Our case was assigned to Judge Royce Lamberth, who was nominated by President Reagan. But as the case progressed, he determined that we needed to go back to the PRRB and have them accept jurisdiction, which they had failed to do initially. The PRRB initially said it did not have jurisdiction. We appealed to the CMS administrator, who found that the PRRB *did* have jurisdiction. We then took the matter up in federal court to resolve the jurisdiction question. The Justice Department argued that the PRRB had jurisdiction, and the court ordered us to go back to the PRRB and obtain a sign-off from them confirming that they did, in fact, have jurisdiction. The court also ruled that the PRRB should grant expedited judicial review (which it eventually did). We believed the ruling reflected Lamberth's belief that the case might be appealed, and he did not want the case to be overturned on a technicality.

The PRRB ultimately agreed that our appeal should be heard in the courts, but we were left with the decision of where we should file our case. We chose Washington, D.C., because any ruling of a D.C.-based federal court would be binding nationwide. And we only contested two fiscal years—2007 (when the error was discovered) and 2008 (when the government changed the reimbursement formula to prevent the error from duplicating). Once we began to move forward with the appeal, the strategy was developed. All cases need to be initiated in the administrative appeals process. In this case, the appeals needed to be filed with the PRRB, which had strict rules for filing appeals, as Chris Keough knew, since he had filed many previous appeals.

When the case began, the needs for filing were limited. Under the rules that existed at the time, the provider needed to assert that it was dissatisfied with its reimbursement and that the impact was greater than $10,000 for a year (or $50,000 for a group of hospitals). The matter also needed to be filed in a timely matter, which was normally within 180 days of the date the hospital received its Notice of Program Reimbursement (NPR). But if appealing an annual rate/rate adjustment, then it was within 180 days of the date of publication of the respective final rule. These NPRs are issued after a review or audit, which is typically about two years after the end of the hospital's fiscal year for that year. Since our appeals generally involved the payment rate, our filings were generally made based upon the rate year. This filing based on the rate year (which is the federal fiscal year) accelerates the time when a year can be filed. A provider with a fiscal year ending September 30, 2007, could file an appeal if it involved a rate-type issue, based on when the final rule for that year was published (usually 60 days prior to the beginning of that fiscal year or approximately August 1, 2006), Accordingly, providers could file180 days after the publication date of the final rule or, in our case, in late January 2007. Alternatively, a provider could also file its appeal based on the date of its NPR, which is usually received after the year is audited or reviewed by Medicare, or about two years after the end of its fiscal year (in this example, that would be around September 30, 2009). Thus, rate year filings accelerate the filings by more than two years, which means more years are included in the appeal pipeline. This was a significant benefit to the hospital in our appeals.

The approach was to file appeals for as many of the initial hospitals as possible, based on the fiscal year 2007 rate, and then work with the hospitals to get their prior years for which NPRs had been issued. Simultaneously with the rate year filings for fiscal year 2007, we began the complicated task of soliciting the hospitals for those open NPR years (their NPRs that were within 180 days of the issuance date). Without a timely issued NPR, the hospitals could also add the rural floor issue to any existing appeals they had on other issues. This was the rule at the initiation of the appeals, but it was subsequently changed to prevent or limit hospitals from adding issues later in the appeal process. The government wanted to limit its liability and preventing hospitals from appealing was a convenient way to do that.

The final rule for the 2007 fiscal year was corrected three times. These corrections meant that the 180-day deadline kept moving forward. Therefore, instead of having to file all the appeals for fiscal year 2007 by the end of January 2007 (180 days after the August 1 publication date of the fiscal year 2007 final rule), it was moved forward another thirty days, until the end of February 2007, and then another thirty days, until the end of March 2007. These extensions gave us more time to solicit hospitals to join our appeal but caused a lot more work because of the volume of appeals that needed to be filed.

# PAPERWORK AS FAR AS THE EYE CAN SEE

The PRRB's appeal process is governed by a specific set of regulatory guidance and timeframes. When the Akin Gump lawyers and I looked at the appeal, we saw ourselves wading through thousands and thousands of pages for each year, for hundreds of hospitals. The workload would be overwhelming and presented the potential for errors if we missed anything.

While Akin Gump had filed numerous large appeals on behalf of clients, the size of this filing would exceed all the others. Fortunately, the firm developed a plan for streamlining the process for us and for the PRRB, which had to handle the same documents we did, as well as a case/data tracking system. The PRRB agreed to this streamlining, which limited the documents needed to three items: (1) an individualized representation letter for each hospital for each year on the hospital's letterhead; (2) the estimated amount being contested (one page); and (3) the four certifications (all on one page, but certifying four different things). This made it possible for virtually all the paperwork to be completed via scanned PDF files in a single package, rather than filing hard copies and live signatures.

Simple, right? Not really. Many hospitals would have their legal counsels review the representation letters and certifications. And then they would change the language in the representation letter and the certifications, despite our declaration that no changes were permitted. With such changes, the documents would not have been acceptable to the PRRB.

As a result, to comply with our agreement with the PRRB, we had to review each piece of paper supplied by each hospital for each year. If there were any differences between documents and the PRRB agreement, we had to go back to the hospital and secure the proper documents. This would frequently involve dealing with the legal counsel of individual hospitals or entire hospital systems. And this process was playing out during a six-week period, with more than seven hundred hospitals. Stressful, to say the least.

But having the representation letters with standardized language describing the issue under appeal gave us the confidence that when the lead case was decided in federal court, there would be no question of its applicability to our other cases not in court.

# IDENTIFYING HOSPITALS AND PLOWING THROUGH MORE PAPERWORK

A second element of our legal strategy was to identify hospital systems to include in the appeal at federal District Court. For candidate hospitals and systems, the payment error clearly needed to be large enough to matter to the affected hospitals, but not so large that a court would think ruling in our favor would threaten the solvency of the Medicare trust fund.

We developed relationships with other consultants who would connect hospitals with us, and we held conference calls, during which we laid out the issues. For those who were interested in joining our appeal, we sent them a letter of agreement that specified the terms of our relationship. (That letter appears in Appendix 4.)

Our initial solicitation of hospitals led to somewhere between 100 and 125 hospitals signing on to the appeal. We weren't sure if we would be able to get any more. Boy, were we wrong. Because of the revisions to the fiscal year 2007 final rule, which included rate adjustments, we continued our solicitation, which brought in another 175 hospitals. A third wave brought in an additional 350 hospitals. This large influx of hospitals, and the labor-intensive administrative procedures is what led to us blowing through the original fee cap.

At the beginning of each one of the federal government's fiscal years, spanning from October 1 to September 30 of each applicable year, we would file appeals within 180 days of the date of publication to the respective final rule. In addition, we were soliciting our hospitals about NPR years and filing those years as well, when applicable. We were typically filing more than seven hundred appeals each year. As a result of the case dragging on for quite some time, we had literally thousands of years under appeal. Processing all the paperwork associated with these appeals, and tracking them, ultimately became quite a burden for us.

Because of the volume and fee cap issues, all the parties involved elected to make appropriate accommodations in their respective agreements and the appeal continued. The initial arrangements with all the parties positioned me as the prover-bial king, meaning I could cease the appeal at any time, without cause or reason. This condition was likely the controlling factor in getting folks to cooperate. As General George Patton once said, "When you have them by the balls, their hearts and minds will follow."

While most of the hospitals and hospital systems signed the agreement letter and didn't quibble over it, the State University of New York (SUNY) system returned it with a lengthy addendum, requesting several absurd changes to the terms. I politely told them this wasn't a negotiation, and we weren't modifying our terms, given that we had more than seven hundred hospitals in our appeal that had essentially the same agreement.

Three years later, a different person from SUNY came back to me and the cycle repeated itself. They wanted in on the appeal, so I sent them a PDF copy, which they could simply sign. They asked for a version of the document in Word, which was a clear signal they were going to make changes to it. We complied and sent a Word version. They sent back an "enhanced" agreement, with twenty pages from their Attorney General's office, including contract requirements for filings with the Secretary of State, and a provision declaring that we wouldn't get any of the settlement until the money was appropriated by the state legislature. The language also indicated that they would have to approve any settlement (something no other hospital requested). We did not agree to this provision, nor any others they wanted, and sent back an agreement we could live with.

A SUNY representative later called me and said, "You don't understand—we are a state hospital system, and the state requires us to include all this language." I told her I did understand. She said, "Then we can put the language back in?" When I said no, she responded, "We need to have it in, don't you understand?" I told her again that I did in fact understand, and added, "What you don't understand is that I'm not signing the agreement with that language in it." She replied, "Then we will not be in your appeal, and we will not get paid" and I said "right." When she said, "That's not fair," I told her, "That's your problem, not my problem."

It's important to note at this time we had 730 hospitals in our appeal, and all had the same basic agreement. The SUNY folks wanted to be an exception, which meant they could have complicated or vetoed the settlement. In addition, at that time, the State of New York had a budget deficit in the billions of dollars, and the language they sought required that there be an appropriation in order for us to get paid. We had similar experiences with other hospitals, and these experiences were reminders of just how inept government officials and hospitals can be. Suffice to say, these obstinate hospital systems were never part of our appeal and, as far as I know, never received a dime from any settlement on our issue.

• • •

As part of our court strategy, we created an initial list of twelve to fifteen small hospital systems. We eventually narrowed it down to just two, and we asked them to be the lead plaintiffs. One was Cape Cod Healthcare, home to more than 450 physicians, 4,700 employees, and 1,100 volunteers, spread across two acute care hospitals, a skilled nursing and rehabilitation facility, an assisted living facility, and homecare and hospice services. Chris Keough had some previous experience with the system, and we were also connected with them through our prior work with the Massachusetts Hospital Association.

The other hospital system was Medisys, a New York-based hospital network that consisted of Jamaica Hospital Medical Center, Flushing Hospital Medical Center, and Brookdale Hospital Medical Center. As of June 2012, Medisys had 6,100 employees, 340,000 outpatient visits annually, and $2.1 billion in annual revenue.

While executives at both Cape Cod and Medisys feared alienating the federal government and wondered about the potential consequences of being the lead plaintiffs in the case, they understood what was at stake and were willing to go forward. And while these two systems, which were essentially five hospitals, served as the lead plaintiffs, the other hospitals stayed at the

PRRB. This independent tribunal has five appointed members, who serve three-year terms, and all administrative appeals regarding Medicare must begin there. It can have hearings on the merits of an issue before it, but not matters of law or statute (which our issue was). Petitioners may request that the PRRB grant Expedited Judicial Review (EJR) in the event the PRRB lacks jurisdiction to grant the relief being sought.

Ultimately, there were nearly 730 hospitals in the appeal. About half of these belonged to hospital systems (with seventy-five systems represented) and the other half were unaffiliated.

We also began the process of estimating the size of the error for each hospital. We had a sense of the size of the error in fiscal year 2007. But we didn't know when the error began. This was critically important because the error was one of duplication and its related compounding effect, so we needed to know the length of time in order to judge the compounding effect.

We initially thought the error had been made by the person or people who did the calculation, given that CMS personnel often moved from one division to another. We hypothesized that the genesis of the error was someone who had moved back and forth and was then doing the calculation. Therefore, we pegged the error initiation to when this individual started doing the calculation, which was around 2004 or 2005, and we based our estimates on that initiation date. But not until we were in federal District Court did we learn the error began much earlier.

Adding to the complexity, the PRRB required hospitals filing appeals in the same group part of the same ownership-controlled group (system) be in the same group. In other words, a separate group for each issue, for each year, and for each system. This meant that we had many system groups of two or three hospitals and some with fifty hospitals for each year that we were filing. All the non-system hospitals could be in the same unaffiliated group. These complex rules increased the administrative burden exponentially considering the vast number of hospitals for which we were filing.

Even greater complexity emerged as a healthcare consulting firm decided to capitalize on our budget neutrality work and began partnering with a law firm (both of which were based in Indiana). It was a large law firm, but at the time it was second or third tier when it came to major litigation. The two firms did not have a good understanding of the rules for filing jurisdictionally proper group appeals. They interpreted them to mean that any system hospitals could be in the same group, even if that group included non-system hospitals. They had fee agreements with the various hospital associations, which we suspected was why they had a group for each year and each state. As I will explain later, the failure of these two entities to follow the PRRB's group rules would eventually catch up with them.

Using a sports analogy, I saw it this way: All of this effort was required just to get us on the field and establish what the game was all about. Whether we'd win the game would be determined later. I eventually concluded that our case was a bit like a game of pool, and we were trying to execute the equivalent of nine-ball combination shot. Any shot we made would have a ricochet effect across the table. In order to prevail, all the nine balls being played would need to strike the next ball with precisely the right amount of force and spin for the object ball to land in the target pocket (other than the eight-ball, of course).

# THE "CHEVRON" STRATEGY

There was one other important dimension to our legal strategy, which rested on a 1984 Supreme Court case, *Chevron v. Natural Resources Defense Council.* In that case, the Court ruled on when to give deference to how a government agency has interpreted a statute it administers. The Court's ruling established what is known as the "Chevron two-step test." The key passages from the decision are as follows:

> *First, always, is the question whether Congress has directly spoken to the precise question at issue. If the intent of Congress is clear, that is the end of the matter; for the court as well as the agency must give effect to the unambiguously expressed intent of Congress.*
>
> *If, however, the Court determines Congress has not directly addressed the precise question at issue, the court does not simply impose its own construction of the statute, as would be necessary in the absence of an administrative interpretation. Rather, if the statute is silent or ambiguous with respect to the specific question, the issue for the court is whether the agency's answer is based on a permissible construction of the statute.*

We wanted the courts to see that the budget neutrality provision was clear and unambiguous, and that CMS had failed to comply with it ("Chevron I"). We knew we would lose if the case rested on making an argument that CMS had botched the budget neutrality calculation relative to the wage index, resulting in a shortfall. Making such an argument would have led the courts to see the issue as one of our numbers versus the government's numbers, and the courts generally defer to the government in situations of an unclear or ambiguous statute. So, the government would counter that, under their calculations, there was no shortfall (or a smaller one), and it would become the government's numbers versus our numbers—"Chevron II."

## SUMMARY

- There were two elements to our legal strategy. One rested on how we wanted our case to move through the appeals process and the legal system. The other was to identify hospital systems for whom to appeal in federal District Court.

- We ended up with nearly 730 hospitals in the appeal—about six times more than we expected.

- A key portion of our legal strategy was showing that the government had failed to comply with the clear and unambiguous budget neutrality provision of the 1997 Balanced Budget Act. If the court saw the issue as the government's numbers versus ours, we would lose.

# 8

# INCOMPETENT COMPETITORS

A s mentioned already, we weren't the only ones pursuing this case. Once I began talking to hospital administrators and CFOs about what we were pursuing, it was inevitable that others in the cloistered world of hospital finance would hear about it. They did, and one of them who ran a consulting firm in Indiana ultimately chose to pursue a parallel effort—trying to round up hospitals and seek retroactive reimbursements from CMS.

This group did not understand the issue, and to this day it still doesn't. Nonetheless, driven by their ego, they wanted to be the standard bearers in challenging the issue. Those who think they know and want to be in charge usually wind up losing and making bad case law.

We viewed the head of this firm as a bottom feeder. Once an appeal issue was identified, he would develop appeals by gaining access to hospitals through their state associations—he had relationships with many of them—to form groups with which to appeal the issue. The state associations would get a cut of the fees his firm received. But the firm would not take on the appeal of the issue itself. Instead, they would stay in the appeal background but make public statements and issue memos that would suggest they were involved in the appeal or litigation.

In the early, formative period, I asked the head of the consulting firm to join our appeal. He declined. His ego was too big, and he needed to portray himself as the lead actor. But letting one's ego get in front of one's *talent* creates a big problem, particularly when it comes to litigation. The arrangements used by his firm tended to call for a three-way split of any settlement, split equally between his firm, the Indiana-based law firm, and the respective hospital association involved.

The consulting firm was making progress in soliciting hospitals through their various association connections until they started to try to market in California. A major law firm in the state was considering something similar and had already discussed the issue with the California Hospital Association. The conflict was resolved with a similar three-way split between the hospital association, the consulting firm, and the California-based law firm.  The consulting firm constructed its basic agreement on a rate-multiplied-by-hours basis for filing the appeals, plus a 10 percent success fee. By comparison, we had a 25 percent success fee, plus a flat fee of $10,000 per hospital, both of which were only payable in the event the appeal succeeded. The consulting firm received its hourly rate fee regardless of whether the appeal was successful or not. This fee differential is why it would have been more lucrative for the consulting firm to join our effort, but the ego of the firm's head interfered.

The individuals at the consulting firm did not understand the core issues involved. Having them on the playing field threatened our ability to succeed in the litigation. Indeed, our efforts could have tanked on several occasions had we not been vigilant about monitoring developments.

One of the many issues triggered by the consulting firm related to the recruitment of hospitals. The head of the firm had relationships with many state hospital associations and signed hospitals up as part of his appeal, even if the hospital had never agreed to appeal the RF-BN issue. But some of the hospitals in these associations had signed on to our appeal and had already certified that they were not in any other appeal for the RF-BN issue for the year involved. If our team and the other team both claimed some of the same hospitals, when these hospitals had signed certifications for us attesting that they had no other appeal on the RF-BN issue for the particular year, then the PRRB could have dismissed both appeals.

The California law firm formed groups for their hospitals and followed the normal course of filing administrative appeals with the PRRB. Like us, they chose to move a group that included virtually all their hospitals for the first two years—fiscal years 2007 and 2008—to the federal District Court in Washington, D.C.

But they, along with the Indiana-based consulting firm and law firm, wanted the limelight and were not content to assist in or support our litigation. The normal protocol is for the principal movers in the matter (the first filed case, which was our appeal in this instance) to retain control and the attorneys from other firms contact the lead firm and offer their assistance (leaving it to the lead firm to accept or reject that offer). These guys were not like that; they demanded center stage regardless of the impact on their clients. Their decision to charge hourly fees could have impacted their desire to keep working (and charging) on the appeal.

In litigation, the government monitors everything that is said and written in the public domain. That's why we said little for six years, but these guys blabbed about *everything*, which often put the litigation in jeopardy. They were putting the interests of their firm ahead of the interests of the hospitals they were representing.

The California-based law firm decided that rather than remain at the administrative level and park their appeals at the PRRB, they would file in the federal District Court for their appealed hospitals for the 2007 and 2008 fiscal years. From the initial case petition, we knew that they did not understand the issues (a given, since they were getting their information from the head of the consulting firm) and that they were unaware of the "smoking gun" email. Even with the email, which eventually became public, they never understood the issue or the email's significance.

What started as a minor distraction evolved into a major obstacle. While all of our attention had been devoted to how we were going to prevail in our fight against the executive branch of the federal government, we eventually needed to turn our attention to how we were going to neutralize these competing legal teams. These folks were unaware of our strategy, and we didn't want them to know, for fear they would do something to mess things up. At one point, we agreed to share our legal briefs with them, in hopes that they would see this as being involved in our effort and not take independent action that would undermine our strategy. It didn't work.

They acknowledged learning from our briefs, but instead of deferring to us, they drew on our briefs to pursue sales pitches with hospitals that might want to sign on to their appeal. The California law firm ultimately did file a case in federal court after our case was in the same court, though their case was assigned to a different judge. At the District Court level, they tried to get our case assigned to their judge. Fortunately, their petition was denied. If successful, this would have subordinated our case to theirs, and they would have been the lead case. Our worst fears were confirmed when one of the partners at the California law firm told Chris that whenever they read one of his briefs, they learned how much they didn't know about this issue. But we were encouraged that Judge Lamberth retained control over the issue, and we saw him as someone who would not be afraid to rule against the executive branch. It was a small victory in a larger— and much, much longer—war.

## SUMMARY

- Another collection of lawyers and consultants pursued a parallel effort to ours, but they did not understand the issue. And they wanted to be the standard bearers in challenging the issue; they were driven by their ego.

- Having them on the playing field threatened our ability to succeed in the litigation. Indeed, our efforts could have tanked on several occasions had we not been vigilant about monitoring developments.

# 9

# THE GOVERNMENT'S STRATEGY

The federal government typically adopts the position that it is not responsible for taking any action before the date they are put on notice of an issue. The date of "public notice" is generally the date a comment letter on the issue is received.

Given the government's action regarding the comment letter, it was clear to us that their strategy was to have our comment letter omitted (the only one ever submitted on the RF error in the fiscal year 2007) from the rulemaking record—as if they had never received it. Therefore, they would have only been responsible (if they were responsible at all) for the damages caused by the error that came *after* the date they were put on notice via court filings or an appeal filed with the PRRB. Thus, the comment letter was a critical piece of the puzzle, as the timing of its existence would determine how much the federal government would ultimately have to pay to the hospitals that had been shortchanged. The government presumably thought that if it succeeded, it would not have been responsible for years prior to 2007, and perhaps not even the compounding effect prior to that date. (The government used "finality" in setting the rate for a year to mean they would never need to pay for prior accumulated effects of any error once the rate was finalized.)

The government's strategy also rested on its claim that the problem had been allegedly fixed. In the 2008 final rule, which was published in August 2007, CMS clarified that it would stop relying on the base payment rate (the cumulative method of achieving BN) and said that, henceforth, it would be relying on adjustments to the wage index to achieve BN. (In other words, they changed how they calculated and applied the RF-BN adjustment.) This changed the method from a cumulative method to a non-cumulative method. The rule announcement included an acknowledgment that "many commenters requested additional information as to the purpose" of the change, but CMS did not provide one. The rule also referenced commenters who had informed CMS of an "inappropriate duplicating effect" created by the calculation of the RF-BN adjustment, but CMS didn't admit to or deny any such error, as is clear in the language below.

> With regard to alleged errors in FYs 1999 through 2007, our calculation of budget neutrality in past fiscal years is not within the scope of this rulemaking. Even if errors were made in prior fiscal years, we would not make an adjustment to make up for those errors when setting rates for FY 2008. It is our longstanding policy that finality is critical to a prospective payment system. Although errors in ratesetting are inevitable, we believe the need to establish final prospective rates outweighs the greater accuracy we might gain if we retroactively recomputed rates whenever an error is discovered.

This focus on "finality" is an established concept in prospective rate-setting regulation. It is the rough equivalent of a statute of limitations—government agencies need to know that after a certain point, they can't be held liable for past mistakes. It's not an unreasonable position, but the government took it to extremes, claiming that making retroactive payment would be forcing the HHS Secretary into making a "Hobson's choice": either violate a statutory directive to maintain budget neutrality or attempt retroactive reductions in the payments made to other providers. Doing either of those things, the government argued, "would likely precipitate more litigation and further erode the finality of previously established rates."

I understood what the government was trying to do, which was to say, in effect, that a ruling in our favor would cause the sky to fall. It was a somewhat persuasive argument (had I been in their position, I might have used it myself) but, as we will learn later, not persuasive enough.

While CMS was digging in its heels on past mistakes, even its supposed "fix" was inadequate. It did nothing to address the fact that the hospitals had been shortchanged for years (an argument we made in the comment letter). The agency did make a one-time transition adjustment to the payment rate. So, while the error ceased duplicating itself, the agency never restored the accumulated effects of all the prior errors. Therefore, *the accumulated effects of the mistake, through the point the agency stopped it from duplicating, were permanently locked into the payment rate.* We were the only ones who realized this. Indeed, the wording in the rule was very unclear and would later be misinterpreted by the federal District Court.* In the fiscal year 2008 rule, CMS described

......................................................................................

* There is legislation/law, regulatory interpretation of law, and case law where courts interpret the law. The courts get the intent of law wrong all the time, which then becomes case law, which is used going forward—wrong decisions become binding.

the new method. It would segregate the RF-BN adjustment from the overall adjustment involving the area wage index, as well as a BN adjustment to a grouping system (known as "diagnosis related groups" or DRG) used to categorize patients for payment or measurement in an acute general hospital. CMS believed this modification would lead to a better result. This was true, but it did not correct the cumulative effects of the methodological error in their RF-BN adjustment that had been in place since 1999. What CMS never said—because it couldn't—was that *the new method would prevent the error from duplicating each year*, which was an admission that duplicating had been occurring in prior years. However, they also wanted to win in court, too, as they did not want to have to pay back the underpayments associated with the error's accumulated effects since 1999.

But why did CMS officials make the change in the first place? They had clearly recognized the error and sought to rectify it, but they did not want to reference the comment letter. The government's federal District Court brief in early 2009 referenced an email it had received (this was my email) that raised the problem to the agency of its calculation of the RF-BN adjustment. But this, too, was a remarkable admission. Strikingly, they were using a simple email as the basis for making a change in the RF-BN calculation, while at the same time arguing in federal court that to be accepted and considered, submitted comments, needed to be properly addressed (more on that momentarily). There was a fundamental contradiction in the government's argument.

# SUMMARY

- The government's strategy was to claim our comment letter had never been received, which is why they omitted it from the rulemaking record based on a delivery technicality.

- CMS fixed its duplicating mistake, but the supposed fix did nothing to address the fact that the hospitals had been short-changed for years. The agency was not restoring the accumulated effects of the prior errors. Therefore, the accumulated effects, through the point they stopped it from duplicating, were permanently locked into the payment rate.

- There was a contradiction in the government's argument. CMS used a simple email as the basis for making a change in the RF-BN calculation, while also arguing that any comments needed to be submitted to the correct address and following a prescribed delivery process.

# 10

# THE SMOKING GUN

A key piece of our strategy was to have our case heard in federal court. We expected that during the discovery process, which is a time early in the case to ask the other side for information, we would ask for the entire rulemaking record, which would reveal the comment letter.

But when CMS provided the rulemaking record, during discovery for the District Court case, the comment letter wasn't included. This was a major problem, since we were the only ones who commented on the issue, and our letter was critical to our appeal. As I note above, a regulatory agency takes the position that it is not liable for claims until it has been put on public notice, which meant, in effect, that the clock wouldn't have started until receipt of a comment letter. And since CMS was allegedly not notified, it believed that it did not need to pay for years prior to the error's discovery in 2006 (and would argue that it would not need to pay for future periods in the event the error was never corrected). CMS knew that we were the sole commenter on this issue, which meant its liability would be greatly diminished if the comment letter would go away.

This began the very important fight over the inclusion of the comment letter into the rulemaking record. While we had sent the email, we had never produced it in any public forum, so it was not expected to be in the record. (It was intentionally left somewhat vague, as we were attempting to avoid telegraphing broadly what we were commenting about.) We then filed motions to make the comment letter part of the public record, using the rationale of the signed receipt. This receipt became a critical document.

On June 9, 2006, I personally hand-delivered our original comment letter and two required copies of the comment letter to the Baltimore office of CMS—plus two extra individually addressed copies (one for each individual involved in the email exchange—Mike and Nina). I chose to hand-deliver the materials myself because I wanted positive proof that it had been received— something I wouldn't get with an electronic submission. The person receiving the materials was a long-time acquaintance of mine and worked in the Division of Acute Care (DAC), in which the comment letter recipients worked. She signed a receipt to acknowledge having received the letters, and even corrected an error I had made in the date—scratching out "2007" and replacing it with "2006." (This acquaintance later claimed in a declaration submitted by CMS to the court that she did not know the submission was a comment letter on a proposed rule, even though the receipt she signed clearly stated the document being submitted was a "Comment Letter to Centers for Medicare and Medicaid Services on the Proposed FY 2007 IPPS Changes.")

Elementary, right? Apparently not. According to the fiscal year 2007 rulemaking record submitted by the HHS Secretary, no comments related to the rural floor had been properly submitted in fiscal year 2007.

# ORIGIN OF AN ERROR

Nina had moved to CMS's Division of Data Services (DDS), though there was nothing untoward about this. It was common for CMS staff to change divisions when seeking to increase their pay grade once a position became open. But her change led us to believe that she could have been the genesis of the error. Perhaps, we thought, when she switched to DDS, and thus had responsibility for the BN calculation, the error became embedded in the RF-BN adjustment. But our theory was incorrect. We later came to believe that she merely started using the prior calculations without rethinking the method, which was an entirely logical thing to do, as she was not aware that there was a need to modify the existing method. In other words, *whoever was doing the calculations during the period between the initial RF year and the second year failed to make a change in the formulas.* And that's when the incorrect formula began duplicating.

But to this day, we think that once Nina received my email, she went to Mike, at which point they knew they had a problem on their hands. And I assume that's why she never responded to my follow-up question. I don't know whether they considered trying to make a correction at this point. Perhaps they did some calculations, in the interest of understanding the size of the error. Whatever the case, I firmly believe they knew they were sitting on a very large error, and not knowing what to do about it, they initially did nothing. I knew that Mike, a GS-15 whose expertise was physician payment systems, had been trying for years to get out of DAC and had only gone there as a favor to the Deputy Director of the Center for Medicare, who was trying to fill a vacancy in the DAC. He had agreed to the position on the condition that he would only stay for a limited time—about two years.

I suspect that once he realized what was stake, he wanted to get out of DAC more urgently. However, he may have thought that departing after an appeal was filed could make it look like he was running from a problem that had emerged on his watch. So, he likely wanted to exit before an appeal was filed (or settled) but didn't know when—or even if—an appeal would be filed. Once it was filed, and he was still in DAC, his strategy—or the strategy of the CMS general counsel—seems to have been to bury the comment letter.

But withholding the comment letter would only work if the Department of Justice (DOJ) didn't know of its existence. Had DOJ known of the letter, it would have been obligated to produce it during discovery. But the letter never surfaced. The dynamic between CMS and DOJ is noteworthy. While DOJ must defend the federal agency in court, it can never be found to be lying or misrepresenting to the court, as that would destroy its credibility in other cases before the courts. My colleagues and I suspected that Mike decided to bury the comment letter because he did not want to be seen as responsible for losing the appeal. It's possible that DOJ became aware of the failure to include the comment letter at about the time we filed in court. We suspect this is when CMS told DOJ what they had done. It's noteworthy that CMS never produced a declaration from Mike denying the comment letter's existence. Instead, the agency resorted to deception, which the judge demolished, as is explained below.

All this mattered because, once the court proceedings began moving forward, burying the letter became a central part of the DOJ/CMS litigation strategy. They knew they needed to keep the comment letter out of the record. Since we were the only ones who had commented, that letter was the only piece of evidence that could be pointed to as placing the agency on notice in June 2006, during the comment period on the fiscal year 2007 rule. Accordingly, that meant they could be held accountable for, and pay for, all the accumulated errors up through that point going forward, and perhaps backward. The error was then at a relatively sizable level, which eventually became capped at that level due to the change in the RF-BN method adopted in fiscal year 2008, as described in the previous chapter. So, they intentionally never produced the letter as part of the rulemaking record. But the government couldn't stipulate that they never received the comment letter, since that would have been a lie.

CMS had previously declared that when hand-delivering a comment letter to the agency, the delivering person should call a specific telephone number. The language in the rule was not worded as a requirement—it was more like a suggestion—though the agency had argued in its briefs that this was a hard requirement.

The best way to fully appreciate the extraordinary lengths to which the government was willing to go to deny the existence of the comment letter is to cite a few passages from a government filing in the case. One claim was that I didn't follow the right procedures:

> [P]laintiffs waived their right to challenge the FY 2007 rule by failing to submit comments in an appropriate manner.... [P]laintiffs did not follow the agency's express, easy-to-follow procedures for commenting on the proposed rule. They instead delivered their comments to an agency employee who

*was not authorized to receive public comments, who was unaware that the materials delivered to her were intended as comments on the rule, and who accordingly did not ensure that the comments were forwarded to the agency's rulemaking staff.*

# THE POWER OF "PLEASE"

Another claim rested on an interpretation of the world "please." Again, the government's brief:

*The proposed rule made plain that, in the case of hand deliveries to the Baltimore office, commenters must call agency rulemaking staff in advance to arrange for delivery. 71 Fed. Reg. 23996 (2006). The court treated this provision as merely optional because the notice asked that commenters "please" call in advance rather than stating that commenters "must" call in advance. Slip op. at 15. This construction of the agency's rule is incorrect. That the agency employed "please" as a "function word to express politeness (see slip op. at 15)" does not make the provision optional. Rather, the use of "please" as a means of more politely informing the public of mandatory requirements is commonplace, familiar to anyone who has been told to "please refrain from smoking" in a hospital or to "please fasten seat belts" on an airplane.*

These claims attracted the attention of Judge Lamberth, as I show below.

One interesting historical detail is that before our appeal was heard by the District Court, we approached the lead counsel at CMS, with whom Chris had a good professional relationship, and offered to settle the case. While we only had a fraction of the hospitals that would eventually join the litigation, we thought we could explain the issue and the case, and also share the smoking-gun email with the CMS general counsel's office. We would also agree to sign a confidentiality agreement that we would not disclose the error to any other parties and not solicit any more hospitals. (We never shared the email because we felt that it would reveal to others the nature and magnitude of CMS's error. But even after the email was ultimately revealed, the competitor law firms still didn't understand the nature of the error.) The CMS counsel curtly replied that a pre-appeal settlement was a "nonstarter." In retrospect, this was an extremely costly mistake, given that we would have settled for a fraction of what the government ultimately paid out and others would not have been able to figure it out and appeal.

## SUMMARY

- In June 2006, I hand-delivered to CMS our original comment letter, spelling out the error in the BN calculation. I received proof of receipt, but once the court proceedings began moving forward, CMS and the DOJ tried to bury the letter, arguing that it had not been received because it was not submitted in an "appropriate manner."

- Part of the government's argument rested on an interpretation of the world "please."

- Before our appeal was even heard by the District Court, we offered to settle with CMS. They rejected our offer. We were prepared to settle for a fraction of what the government ultimately paid out.

# 11

# THE DISTRICT COURT DECIDES

In court proceedings involving the federal government, the Department of Justice represents all federal agencies. Because the department's attorneys go before the courts on many issues, they will not say anything intentionally wrong. But they can mislead through creative wordsmithing, which often needs to be rebutted in some manner.

That was the backdrop to the initial filings during discovery. The government did not contest our claim and thereby agreed with how we characterized the agency's method of performing the BN calculation. In other words, CMS acknowledged having botched the RF-BN reimbursement formula from its inception. However, in its final brief, the government implied that CMS had corrected its past mistake via the one-time adjustment in the fiscal year 2008 rulemaking, though this ignored that the formula had been wrongly applied since the initial implementation in 1999. What the government never addressed in that brief (because it did not want to) was its failure to make any corrective measure to compensate those institutions that had been shortchanged by the flawed formula. Nor did the government correct the rate *prospectively* to account for the total impact of the error. Essentially, it was hiding behind the "finality" concept.

The litigation was an opportunity to have a judge rule on one of the remarkable aspects of this saga: the federal government's attempt to deny ever having received the comment letter I submitted to CMS in June 2006. Judge Lamberth forcefully rejected the government's claim, as shown in the following passage from his decision:

> In the CMS proposed rule instructions for submitting comments via hand delivery, the instructions told commenters: "If you intend to deliver your comments to the Baltimore address, please call telephone number (410) 786-7195 in advance to schedule your arrival with one of our staff members." While it is clear Mr. Giovanis did not call the telephone number listed, the purpose of calling the number was to schedule arrival with "one of" CMS's staff members prior to dropping off the comment. This is precisely what Giovanis did. The comment was properly addressed and hand-delivered to the address given in the notice. Further, Giovanis called a staff member responsible for PPS payment policies and arranged for his arrival. Giovanis also submitted the two additional copies of the comment letter, as required by the instructions. The Secretary asserts that the comments must be excluded because Mr. Giovanis failed to call the exact number as listed in the Federal Register. However, Mr. Giovanis called a staff member and, in any event, the government argument fails because the agency accepted the comments in fact, as indicated on the time-stamped acceptance of the comments. By

honoring the scheduled arrival of Giovanis and accepting the comments, the government indicated that Giovanis's submission was acceptable.

Further, the plain language of the Federal Register request informs prospective commenters that calling the specific telephone number listed is not required. The instructions state to "please call" in advance. The use of the word "please" evinces the agency's intent to make the instruction recommended, rather than mandatory. See Webster's Ninth New Collegiate Dictionary 903 (1990) (defining "please" as "used as a function word to express politeness or emphasis in a request"). If the agency intended to make this provision mandatory, it would have stated as such. For example, in directing commenters that there is only one address to submit comments via overnight or express mail, the agency stated that "[y]ou may send written comments [...] to the following address ONLY."

The Secretary contends that even though the letter has "a supposed acknowledgement of receipt by a CMS employee, that signature is insignificant [...] to authenticate the letter" because the letter cannot be found in CMS files. This argument must fail. If taken to its logical conclusion, whenever the government misplaces a file, it could claim that it simply never existed. This result would be absurd. Therefore, the Court concludes that the e-mail exchange between Mr. Giovanis and CMS staff members was properly excluded from the FY 2007 rulemaking record. However, the formal comments submitted by Mr. Giovanis were improperly excluded from the FY 2007 rulemaking record.

There's one other fact that underscores the government's duplicity related to the comment letter. While they claimed not to have received it, and thus didn't include it in the rulemaking record, they claimed in a March 2009 memorandum for summary judgment that they had fixed the problem in response to our email, acknowledging that the change had been "triggered in part by this email exchange." This was a key concession, and the passage merits being reproduced in full:

*In May 2006, a CMS employee received an email inquiry from a hospital consultant, Theodore Giovanis, requesting specific details of how CMS calculated the rural floor budget neutrality adjustment. R08:493. Another CMS employee responded on behalf of CMS and explained that CMS performed the calculation for the coming year by comparing estimated payments using the old (current year's) wage data without the rural floor to the new (coming year's) wage data with the rural floor. R08:492. Mr. Giovanis then replied to the CMS employee's email by raising a question about whether this method might "duplicate in some respects" other aspects of the rural floor application. R08:492.*

*While Mr. Giovanis' email was submitted during the time period when the FY 2007 IPPS rulemaking process was underway, it was not submitted as a comment on the FY 2007 Proposed Rule, and the time constraints involved did not allow CMS to take up the issue sua sponte during the FY 2007 rulemaking process.* However, triggered in part by

---

* The following footnote appeared in the government's memorandum: "This fact can be inferred from the absence of the email exchange from the FY 2007

Continued on page 91

*this email exchange, CMS did take a new look at the § 4410
rural floor budget neutrality requirement after the FY 2007
rule had been issued. As a result of this new look, in its Proposed Rule for FY 2008, CMS proposed a prospective change
in its methodology for implementing the rural floor budget
neutrality adjustment. R08:9, 109 (72 Fed. Reg. 24680 (May
3, 2007)). Under the new methodology, CMS would apply
the budget neutrality adjustment factor to the wage index
rather than to the standardized amount. R08:109-10. The
adjustment factor would be calculated by using FY 2006
discharge data and comparing simulated payments using
FY 2008 post-rural floor wage indexes to those using FY
2008 pre-rural floor wage indexes. R08:114. CMS stated its
"belie[f] that the statute supports either an adjustment to
the standardized amount or the wage indexes because under
either methodology, the rural floor would not result in aggregate payments that were greater or less than those that would
have been made in the absence of a rural floor." R08:114.
In connection with this change, CMS also proposed a one-
time 1.002214 "rural floor adjustment" to the standardized
amount. R08:161. CMS solicited and received comments on
this proposed methodological change. R08:494-1332.*

. . . . . . . . . . . . . . . . . . . . . . . . . . . . . . . . . . . . . . . . . . . . . . . . . . . . . . . . . . . . . . . . . . . . . . . . . . . . . . . . . . .

rulemaking record, which indicates that the email was not under consideration
by the agency for purposes of the FY 2007 rulemaking process. The inclusion of
the email exchange in the FY 2008 rulemaking record indicates that the email
exchange did play a role in CMS's decision to take a fresh look at the § 4410(b)
adjustment after the FY 2007 rule was issued, which ultimately led to CMS's
proposal in the FY 2008 rulemaking process."

# THE COURT DECISION

Judge Lamberth ruled in our favor that the government had "improperly excluded" our comment letter from the fiscal year 2007 rulemaking record. However, on the broader issue, he ruled against us because he thought the error was corrected by the one-time adjustment. This was a huge blow, and we were devastated by the defeat. We did a lot of soul-searching to try to determine why we lost. Was it our brief? Was it the judge? Or something else altogether?

We presented a very strong case, but it was all in writing—the judge did not allow oral arguments. And we were handicapped by not having the opportunity to rebut the government's arguments (as the plaintiff, we presented our arguments first). In the DOJ's brief, it implied that CMS had retroactively corrected its past duplication error, given that the fiscal year 2008 rulemaking prevented the error from further duplication. But the correction only applied to the future. In other words, *it didn't address the past underpayments that were already built into this payment rate, and this was at the heart of our case*. We suspect that the DOJ meant to be misleading, and we came to believe that Judge Lamberth misinterpreted DOJ's brief, which led him to rule against us.

As I noted in Chapter 9, in the fiscal year 2008 final rule, CMS adopted its proposal to modify adjustments to the RF-BN methodology. Previously, the RF-BN adjustment had always been to the payment rates and, accordingly, was perpetual in nature. Once the incorrect adjustment in this case had been made to the rate, it was never removed. The government's modification of the methodology in the fiscal year 2008 rule moved the RF-BN adjustment from the payment rate to the area wage index (AWI).

(The AWI-based method kept the error from duplicating, as it was a new calculation each year, and therefore any adjustment incorporated into the AWI would apply only for that year.)

• • •

This change, once proposed, told us that CMS knew about the error, but did not want to be held responsible for (and have to pay for) any of the errors that were incorporated into the rate prior to when the agency was theoretically notified. These prior errors represented all the accumulated effects of the error through 2008, when they changed the method.

When CMS discussed the adjustment in the rule, it skirted the issue of why the adjustment was made and never implied anything was wrong. Instead, CMS made a so-called "one-time" add-back to the payment rate. We believed this confused Judge Lamberth. The DOJ's brief in this area also implied that the problem was fixed. Yes, the duplication was going to end, but that was not the entire issue.

There were two problems in play: the method that was duplicating *and* the accumulated effects of all the prior errors that were in the payment rate. The fix *did* stop the error from being duplicated under the new AWI-based RF-BN method. The fix *did not* address the need for repayment of all the previously accumulated errors now in the rate—past or future—which was the fundamental issue in the appeal.

But it wasn't a total defeat. Judge Lamberth allowed our original comment letter to be included in the rulemaking record of fiscal year 2007. This established that CMS had been put on notice that it had made a mistake, and thus started the clock earlier than CMS wanted. And that meant that if we ever prevailed, the size of CMS's miscalculation would be much larger. This was a big deal—a *very* big deal.

We weren't sure why Lamberth allowed the letter to be included, because if he believed the government had fixed its past mistake, the comment letter would have been irrelevant. Our theory—and it was only a theory—was he might have suspected he was wrong and wanted to give us some ammunition if we were going to appeal.

It's understandable that Lamberth would be confused. Both Graham and I are Medicare experts, and even we had to devote many hours, over a period of weeks, to conclude with absolute certainty that the fiscal year 2008 change was incomplete. In reality, this add-back was only an adjustment that compensated for the change in the method used for the RF BN—from the cumulative method to the non-cumulative method. (Thus, the Medicare adjustment only prevented the error from continuing to duplicate in future years.) The total amount for the error remained in the base rate and would have been locked into that rate had we not continued to pursue the case. We were the only ones that figured this out and made the case in comments and in our legal briefs.

We knew from the beginning that we faced an uphill fight, but we were convinced we had the facts on our side, and so we had prepared an appeal just in case we lost. When we did lose, we filed our appeal with the U.S. Court of Appeals for the D.C. Circuit the next day.

After losing in the District Court, Ron, our financier, wanted me to try reaching an agreement with the government to settle. I told him that the government would have no interest in settling, as they would want to wait for the Court of Appeals decision. But he pushed and pushed and threatened to call Andrew Cuomo, the Governor of New York, and get him to call President Obama about the matter. Ron was a close friend of Cuomo (and his father, Mario), so I had no doubt he could reach him. While I did not believe that an appeal from Cuomo would lead President Obama to get involved, I still didn't think it was a good idea for Ron to make the call—and I told him that. The team and I believed that any interference from the outside would work against the hospitals. If Cuomo—or any other governor—believed that the hospitals in their state were going to get a windfall of cash, the first thing they would do is look for a way to reduce the state's Medicaid rates to get some or all of that windfall. So, I wound up yelling at Ron, "No, you are not going to call them!" He responded, "Yes I am!" And I responded, "No, you're not."

In the end, both Ron and I knew that my agreement with him specified that I had the sole right to prosecute and settle the appeal, so if he called Cuomo against my direction not to, he could be in violation of our agreement, and I could be justified in refusing to pay him any portion of the settlement. He relented and never placed the call.

## SUMMARY

- The District Court ruled in our favor that the government had "improperly excluded" our comment letter from the fiscal year 2007 rulemaking record. But on the broader issue, it ruled against us because it thought the error was corrected by the one-time adjustment.

- Our team believed that the judge who presided over the case misinterpreted the brief submitted by the Department of Justice. But the judge allowed our original comment letter to be included in the rulemaking record of fiscal year 2007. This established that CMS had been put on notice that it had made a mistake, and thus started the clock earlier than the CMS wanted. This was a *very* big deal.

- One day after we lost the case, we filed an appeal.

# 12

# VICTORY IN THE COURT OF APPEALS

As we were preparing for the oral argument at the Court of Appeals, which was scheduled to begin in late 2010, Chris called me with an idea. He proposed that one of his King & Spalding colleagues, Paul Clement, argue the case. He explained that Clement had been U.S. Solicitor General and had sixty Supreme Court oral arguments to his credit. I was intrigued, but I wanted to meet him first.

While Clement's credentials were unimpeachable, I was nonetheless concerned, given the complexity of the issues at stake, as well as the numeric calculations that were involved. Whoever argued our case needed to possess a comprehensive understanding of the issues *and* be able to explain it in layman's terms to the judges.

I met with Clement about a week later, and although he had read the briefs, neither Chris nor Steph had walked him through the issues. But after about twenty-five minutes, I knew he was the right guy to argue the case. He had quickly grasped what was at stake, and he had developed some ideas about how to argue the case with the court.

In the brief the legal team submitted to the court, we specified that we were challenging two budget years, 2007 and 2008, on the grounds that HHS—CMS's parent agency—had miscalculated the adjustment to the standardized amount such that hospitals were being systematically underpaid and BN was not achieved. Moreover, because the error affected the standardized amount, which is carried over from year to year, the errors compounded over time. The appeal included the fiscal year in which the error was identified (2007) as well as the fiscal year in which the CMS asserted change in the RF-BN method and its alleged correction (2008). The brief stated the following:

*In 2007, the Appellant Hospitals pointed out this error to the Secretary, and she did nothing. Budget year 2007 thus presents a particularly clear case of administrative action that is contrary to law. The Secretary flatly violated the statutory directive to adjust the wage index and failed to achieve budget neutrality. For the 2008 budget year, the Secretary finally adjusted the correct component of the reimbursement formula, but she still failed to achieve budget neutrality. While she stopped making one error, she did not correct the standardized amount to account for the fact that it had been incorrectly deflated over prior years by her miscalculations. The Secretary's use of that distorted number in 2008 failed to produce budget neutrality in 2008. The errors in both 2007 and 2008 must be remedied.*

Later in the brief, the attorneys went into more detail about how the HHS Secretary had abrogated her duties:

*For nearly a decade, the Secretary violated the plain text of § 4410(b) by ignoring its clear directive to "adjust the area wage index" to account for the payment effect of the rural floor, and instead adjusting the standardized amount. If the Secretary had followed Congress' directive, the issue here would never have arisen—the wage index is calculated anew each year, so the adjustments would have had to be noncumulative, and could not possibly have resulted in duplication from year to year. Nonetheless, the Secretary's deviation from Congress' directive would not have affected the regulated community if she had correctly adjusted the standardized amount through the "cumulative" approach she told the world she was using. But the Secretary was not using a cumulative approach. Instead, she was using a method that was neither fish nor fowl—an incoherent combination of the two methods that improperly reduced payments to hospitals by repeatedly duplicating the payment effect of the rural floor each year and then carrying over the improperly reduced standardized amount from year to year.*

Oral arguments began on November 8, 2010. The presiding judge was David Tatel (a liberal) and joining him were Stephen Williams (a conservative) and A. Raymond Randolph (a conservative who knew Clement well). We didn't know what to expect, but we were confident we had the facts on our side. I was in the courtroom as an observer, as were Chris, Steph, and my former associate, who had been involved with the appeal from the beginning.

Our side presented first (as plaintiffs customarily do), and I thought our brief persuasively laid out the facts of the case. Each attorney is only allowed fifteen minutes to present; however, there is no time limit on responding to questions from the justices. Clement started by saying he wanted to preserve one-and-a-half minutes of his time for rebuttal. He'd only been speaking for about thirty seconds when the justices started pummeling him with rapid-fire questions. They just kept coming and coming. In the end, Clement only had twenty-five seconds for rebuttal. I had a bad feeling about where this was going to wind up.

But my mood brightened once Jeffrey Clair, the Department of Justice attorney handling the case, began his oral argument. Almost immediately, the judges also started pummeling him with questions—and their apparent skepticism was a few notches higher than anything directed at Clement. Six minutes into Clair's presentation, I wrote a note to one of those attendance: "This guy wants this over in the worst way."

We initially thought the error began in 2004 or 2005, but during the District Court case we learned it started in 1999. This made a big difference to the size of the error, which we emphasized in the brief submitted to the Court of Appeals. A table summarizing a hypothetical example appeared in our brief (see next page).

One member of our legal team, John Faust, had also devised a hypothetical example that we all thought the judges would be able to understand. It involved a company giving one of its employees a car and how that would impact the employee's compensation under the government's application method of "budget neutrality." The court seemed to like this example and quoted from it at length.

*Imagine an employee normally earns $10 per hour. His employer decides to give him a company car, the value of which equates to compensation of $1 per hour. To avoid*

## THE POWER OF COMPOUND GROWTH

*An illustration of how the magnitude of the error grew over time*

| Year | Annual Effect of RF | Annual RF Adjust. to SA | Cumulative RF Adjust. to SA | Annual Payment Effect of Cum. RF Adjs. | Annual Under-Payment | Total Under-Payment |
|------|------|------|------|------|------|------|
| '98 | $100M | (.002) | (.002) | ($100M) | 0 | 0 |
| '99 | $100M | (.002) | (.004) | ($200M) | $100M | $100M |
| '00 | $100M | (.002) | (.006) | ($300M) | $200M | $300M |
| '01 | $100M | (.002) | (.008) | ($400M) | $300M | $600M |
| '02 | $100M | (.002) | (.010) | ($500M) | $400M | $1.0B |
| '03 | $100M | (.002) | (.012) | ($600M) | $500M | $1.5B |
| '04 | $100M | (.002) | (.014) | ($700M) | $600M | $2.1B |
| '05 | $100M | (.002) | (.016) | ($800M) | $700M | $2.8B |
| '06 | $100M | (.002) | (.018) | ($900M) | $800M | $3.6B |
| '07 | $100M | (.002) | (.020) | ($1.0B) | $900M | $4.5B |

*an increase in the employee's overall compensation—i.e.,
to achieve "budget neutrality"—the employer reduces the
employee's wage to $9 per hour. Now imagine that next year,
the employee receives a nicer car worth $2 per hour. To cal-
culate what the employee's wage should then be to keep his
overall compensation at $10 per hour, the employer could
use either a cumulative or noncumulative approach. Under
the cumulative method, the employer would subtract the $1
incremental increase in the value of the car from the employee's current wage of $9 to arrive at a new, budget-neutral
wage of $8. Under the noncumulative approach, the employer
would simply subtract the full value of the car ($2) from
the desired total compensation ($10) to arrive at the same
figure—a wage of $8 per hour. But it would make no sense
for the employer to subtract the full $2 value of the new
car from the employee's current $9 wage and thus pay him
only $7 per hour. Doing so would not be "budget neutral"—it
would reduce the employee's total compensation by $1 per
hour. Yet this is essentially what the hospitals accuse CMS
of doing in calculating the annual budget-neutrality adjustment to account for the rural floor. Specifically, the hospitals
argue that CMS has duplicated prior adjustments by each
year calculating the full amount of the adjustment necessary
to counteract the effect of the rural floor and then applying
that adjustment to a figure that includes adjustments carried
over from previous years.*

Judge Tatel asked Clair to respond to this explanation of BN, which
we took as a very good sign. Clair fumbled for an explanation
and ultimately evaded the question altogether. Tatel also asked

Clair a hypothetical question about BN, based on our example, and Clair again fumbled in his answer. When Tatel asked again, Clair fumbled yet again, and when Tatel asked a *final* time, Clair suggested a different hypothetical. Tatel cut him off: "No, no, no. Don't change the example on me. Please." This meant that Tatel understood our brief's example and wanted Clair to debunk his understanding. Tatel was giving Clair a chance.

The judges asked a lot of technical questions, and one of them, Judge Randolph, conceded that the material was "so abstract as to really be almost incomprehensible." There was an extended discussion of the comment letter, with the judges expressing skepticism about the CMS official failing to record its receipt. Judge Tatel asked, "Do you think it's likely that she just threw it away?" Clair replied, "I think what's likely is she took the package not realizing that it was a comment, that somehow it got lost somewhere in the Agency."

Once the hearing ended, our group was confident we'd have Tatel and Williams on our side. And while that was all we needed for victory, we weren't sure about Randolph. Clement had noticed that in one of the cases being heard before ours that day Randolph had asked two questions about facts in the case that were already addressed in the respective brief, which suggested he might have been having an off-day or was not fully prepared. But we wanted a unanimous decision, because that would undermine the likelihood of the government appealing to the full circuit court (all the judges of the circuit) or to the Supreme Court.

Immediately after the oral argument, the nine members of our team caucused. We all said it was two in favor, and we all identified the same two—one of them a liberal who generally ruled in favor of the government, and one of them a conservative with a propensity to rule against the government. I mention this because judges often meet immediately after a hearing to discuss how it went and how they might rule. If there is consensus, they can determine which judge will write the majority opinion. Keough and I went back to Akin Gump's office for debriefing, and I called my wife, Jayne, to update her. There was no real celebration—just a sense of positivity, coupled with speculation about when a decision would come. Since nothing is certain when dealing with the government or the courts, we also discussed our thinking on an appeal to the full circuit if the decision went against us. I later asked Clement how he put up with the pummeling from the judges. He simply said, "It comes with the turf. You get used to it."

Our post-hearing outlook proved accurate. On January 14, 2011, the Court of Appeals issued a unanimous decision in favor of our lead group of hospitals. The decision's wording used many parts from our briefs and was definitively in our favor.

The judges shot down CMS's argument that it wasn't going to make changes to the past funding because "finality is critical to a prospective payment system" and "calculation of budget neutrality in past fiscal years [was] not within the scope of th[e] [2008] rulemaking." According to the judges, "This response to the commenters' concerns is insufficient for two reasons."

*First, CMS's interest in the finality of prospective payment rates cannot justify failing to correct past errors in calculating rural-floor budget-neutrality adjustments that affect the aggregate amount of current Medicare payments. Second, the agency's interest in finality fails to address the hospitals' contention that in transitioning from a cumulative to a noncumulative system, CMS needed to reverse all prior rural-floor*

*budget-neutrality adjustments to the standardized amount
even if those adjustments had been calculated correctly.*

The key passage in the decision was the following:

*[The] hospitals have made a compelling argument that
regardless of whether CMS made computational errors in
calculating the rural-floor budget-neutrality adjustments for
years preceding 2008, it should have reversed all of those
prior adjustments in transitioning to its new system of making
noncumulative adjustments to the wage index. CMS failed
adequately to address this concern in issuing its 2008 final
rule. Furthermore, the rationale that CMS did provide—that
its interest in finality justifies its refusal to revisit previously
calculated rural-floor budget-neutrality adjustments—fails on
its own terms because BBA section 4410(b) does not permit
the agency to ignore prior errors in calculating rural-floor
budget-neutrality adjustments when those errors are built
into the formula used to calculate current Medicare payments.*

In other words, the regulatory processes do not override the
agency's requirement to comply with a clear statutory directive
to achieve BN.

The judges also rejected the argument by the Secretary of
Health and Human Services that the error could be overlooked
because it was in the past.

*[In] both her response to comments regarding the 2008 rule
and her brief on appeal, the Secretary has invoked what*

*might be called the "Mark McGwire defense," seeking to avoid the potential consequences of the mistakes the hospitals allege CMS has made by repeatedly asserting that she is "not here to talk about the past." [...] ("With regard to alleged errors in [fiscal years] 1999 through 2007, our calculation of budget neutrality in past fiscal years is not within the scope of th[e] [2008] rulemaking.") This will not do. Having built the past into the cumulative methodology it chose for counteracting the budgetary impact of the rural floor, CMS may not now ignore past errors that have the effect of overly deflating current aggregate payments in violation of BBA section 4410(b)'s budget-neutrality mandate. To the extent the Secretary argues that the Medicare statutes authorize or require CMS to carry over from year to year erroneously calculated rural-floor budget-neutrality adjustments to the standardized amount, her interpretation of the statutes is not a "permissible construction" entitled to Chevron deference. Chevron, U.S.A., Inc. v. Natural Res. Def. Council, Inc., 467 U.S. 837, 843 (1984). Congress has required only that the standardized amount be carried over annually (with appropriate adjustments for inflation). See 42 U.S.C. § 1395ww(d) (3)(A)(iv)(II). The Secretary points to no statutory provision requiring rural-floor budget-neutrality adjustments to the standardized amount to be carried over in this manner. Indeed, in promulgating the 2008 final rule, which itself reversed the 2007 rural-floor budget-neutrality adjustment, CMS seems to have recognized the absence of any statutory bar to reversing the effect of prior rural-floor budget-neutrality adjustments. If, as the Secretary seems to suggest, prior adjustments to the standardized amount are sacrosanct, it is difficult to understand how CMS could have made this small corrective adjustment in 2008.*

Fundamental to our victory was overcoming the deference that's typically shown to the government, particularly in matters as complex as this one. If the dispute was simply about their calculation versus our calculation, the government was going to prevail. But when the government acknowledged that it performed the BN calculation the way we said it did, and thus had violated the statute, that made it possible for the judges to rule in our favor.

The Court of Appeals sent the case back to federal District Court, which in turn remanded the case back to the Secretary of Health and Human Services to either explain why she did not consider our initial comment letter in developing the fiscal year 2007 rulemaking or recalculate the 2007 and 2008 fiscal years' payments for the hospitals, using a formula that would remove the effects of the prior RF-BN adjustments. (These were the only two years in the Cape Cod case, but which applied to all fiscal years prior to 2012, which was when the government ultimately agreed to restitution for the full amount of its past error in future rates.)

I learned of the decision while sitting in my home office, via an email from Chris and Steph. I was elated and felt a sense of vindication. But I also knew, in football terms, we weren't yet in the end zone. For the hospitals to get paid—and thus for me and our partners to get paid—we would have to reach a settlement with the government. And I knew that could be an arduous process, with no guarantee of a large payout—or even *any* payout.

In May 2011, CMS issued a proposed rule for fiscal year 2012, but it did not include an add-back to the payment rate. This timeframe coincided with our settlement discussions with

CMS, which included our ability to calculate how hospitals had been impacted by the payment errors—no easy task. Based on our calculations about the amount of the error, we knew the add-back should be about a 1.1 percent addition onto the payment rate—or about $1.1 billion in aggregate payments per year going forward.

## SUMMARY

- We selected former U.S. Solicitor General Paul Clement to argue our case before the Court of Appeals. His performance was superb, though we also had a strong set of briefs, which included a hypothetical example of how BN could be violated.

- The three judges who heard the case ruled unanimously in our favor and quoted extensively from our briefs.

# 13

# TRYING TO REACH A SETTLEMENT

E ven with the favorable ruling, the drama did not end. Indeed, it escalated. The fundamental issue was simple: reaching a settlement with the government. Getting there was anything but simple. More than six months passed before CMS would truly begin talking with us. At one point I asked Chris what they were doing. "Trying to control the terms of their own surrender," he replied.

Our goal was to get our clients as much money as possible, as soon as possible. We weren't thinking much about the two law firms and the consulting firm, though we were open to playing hardball with them since they never really cooperated with us. If anything, they obstructed us, and we had to overcome (and rehabilitate from) damage they caused.

The other law firms were trying to accelerate the settlement process from the very beginning, even if doing so was not in the best interests of all their clients or ours. The California-based law firm wanted everything settled by the end of the first quarter of 2012, even if the settlement and the related payment amounts due to their clients from the government had not been calculated. We knew that trying to rush the settlement would give the government the upper hand and likely lead to hospitals getting shortchanged.

And those law firms were relentless. They enlisted several large accounting firms to pummel me with requests about when the settlement would occur so they could "book" it. These firms enlisted some of my own clients, who called me and made the same request. It was like an infection that was spreading. There was just one problem: we were still negotiating the settlement terms with the government right up until the very end of March 2012, and verification of amounts due followed.

So, why were they all so intent on securing a settlement in the first quarter? Two of the parties in the California-based law firm's appeal were two hospital companies, both of which were large, publicly traded operators of hospitals and health systems throughout the country. And both were facing Medicare-related fraud charges that were going to mean take-backs in the first quarter of 2012. (When a company faces take-backs, Medicare subtracts from a hospital's biweekly payment the amount the hospital is judged to owe Medicare.) Those take-backs would depress each company's earnings per share and potentially reduce their stock price, and thus adversely affect senior executives and other large holders of the company stock as well as the company's stockholders. Accordingly, the lead lawyer at the California-based law firm, provoked by their clients, wanted to include the settlement in the first quarter to offset the impact of the fraud take-back. If that meant their other clients suffered in the process, so be it.

While I managed our attorneys, I was not *one* of them. (I don't have a law degree, but I do understand law.) But because

under my agreements with the hospitals I was solely in charge—
strategy being one of my strengths—I had the right to act in ways
that were probably a bit different than what they were accus-
tomed to. They quickly came to respect my role and judgment,
particularly since it was my decision to move forward with an
appeal following the loss at the District Court. I also kept the legal
team mostly intact after the loss; they said other clients would
have thrown them under the bus.

• • •

Another example of how the other firms were playing by different
rules than we were emerged during the appeals process. First,
some background.

The PRRB's rules for filing group appeals are called CIRP rules
(Common Issue Related Party). The issue being appealed must be
common or the same for all the hospitals. The hospitals must be
related by common ownership or control and the amount being
contested must exceed $50,000 for the group—an easy thresh-
old. These hospitals must be in the same "common" group for a
given year.

If a system has two hospitals, for example, then those two
hospitals must be in their own group for the single common issue
for that year. Similarly, if the system has fifty hospitals, then all
fifty must be in their own separate group for any given year. We
had seventy-five groups for each year under appeal. Most of our
appeals were for 2007, 2008, 2009, 2010, and 2011, though for
some groups the appeals reached as far back as 2000. Therefore,
we had *hundreds* of groups. All the hospitals that were not affiliated by common ownership or control could be placed in one

large group for the year, provided the issue was common and the hospitals satisfied all the other filing requirements. These were the rules to which we strictly adhered to avoid complications at the PRRB and running the risk of having an appeal dismissed.

However, one of the other firms did not pursue things this way. They had structured their financial relationship through the various state hospital associations. Therefore, their initial filings grouped all the hospitals in each state. This allowed them to keep the associations separate, as those associations received a portion of the fees that were to be paid by those hospitals. But they were ignoring the PRRB rules in the process and exposing their clients to risks.

One of the other firms also took the position that the CIRP rules were applied such that the hospitals under common ownership were in the same group, even though there were many other hospitals in that same group. But that was a violation of the CIRP rules. The PRRB brought this to their attention—creating a major problem for them and requiring significant effort to resolve.

The PRRB ordered the firm to remedy the situation—no small task, by any means. Chris described it best: "It's hard to unscramble an egg once it's scrambled." Refiling the incorrectly filed appeals would have involved enormous amounts of time and energy. In the end, they were able to negotiate a resolution with the PRRB that they would file the appeals correctly going forward but could allow the previously filed appeals to remain that way. Further complicating matters, as the appeal process was ongoing, the hospital industry was in a very dynamic state. Hospitals were being acquired by systems and individual hospitals were combining to form systems. It was like Monte Hall's *Let's Make a Deal*.

As this activity was occurring, the PRRB groups and other

appeal rules were changing. To stay on top of this, we changed how we solicited information from hospitals. In addition, we constantly reminded hospitals that they needed to tell us if—and when—things were going to change.

Amid this wrangling, we still had to keep the pressure on the government, which had every incentive to drag out the payment process. To buy time, the government will sometimes argue that the settlement process is administratively complicated and they need to work through fiscal intermediaries under the Medicare program. And the courts will often give the government a year or more to settle or resolve a case.

We decided to begin the very laborious and time-consuming process of moving all our cases from the PRRB (where they had been for all years) to the District Court. (The exceptions were the five hospitals in the FY-2007 and FY-2008 court cases.) By this time, there were thousands of individual hospital and group appeals in our appeal. As more hospitals appealed, often involving multiple years, more paper and more forms were generated, which increased the likelihood of error. Nevertheless, we started the process because we knew it was necessary to resolve the matter. We also knew it was best for our clients. Having the appeals in court meant that all the appeals would be subject to any related court order and interest on amounts due accrues—an incentive for the government to pay to avoid a payout increase. By contrast, the two other law firms chose not to move all their cases to courts, thereby exposing themselves and their clients to risk, but at the same time saving themselves time and effort.

The settlement agreements were completed on April 2, 2012, and they became public shortly thereafter, though there was no mention of the payment amounts to each hospital nor the total payout. And the settlement didn't attract much attention. One article in the *Los Angeles Times* focused on the California hospitals that were part of the settlement and quoted a CMS official saying the agency had agreed to the settlement "to resolve potential liability associated with an alleged error in calculating inpatient hospital rates." I was struck that, even after the settlement, CMS was still refusing to concede mistakes or "potential liability"—saying that error was "alleged." They never admit wrongdoing.

At this point, we were given two options. All groups could submit a spreadsheet to the government specifying what each hospital was owed for each year (essentially, a large file of amounts due by year aggregated into a single total by hospital), and then our numbers would be checked by CMS. Or the government could calculate what it thought each hospital was owed and have the groups check the numbers. The government preferred the first option because that meant paying the hospitals amounts that the hospitals themselves determined, rather than the government. This would make it more difficult for the hospitals to object to the amounts later since they were the ones who determined those amounts. At the request of the DOJ, we had drafted both settlement agreements—our numbers and CMS's. We eventually got the two law firms and the consulting firm to buy into the agreement we drafted.

From the beginning, we opted to do the calculations based on formulas we developed, which were calculated by DataGen, so we could determine how much each hospital was owed. This meant that we knew the amounts due for all hospital nationally, which included the hospitals in the appeals of the other law firms. This was an extremely labor-intensive exercise, as it meant we had to rerun the claims for each year, using a formula that compensated via adjustments for all the adjustments that would be in the Medicare amounts. There were many iterations.

We had developed two approaches for calculating the amounts that were due—one was top-down and the other was bottom-up. Both came close to one another. We ultimately settled on the bottom-up approach, which we used to provide the amounts to the government. These amounts were calculated for only the years that had been appealed and used the error factors for the respective years.

Our negotiating strategy was to focus on the years after 2007, since the error was the greatest in those years. We were willing to accept a discount for the prior years for three reasons: (1) The dollar amounts were smaller, since the error had been accumulating for fewer years; (2) There were not many such years; (3) Arguing about these years could lead the government to hold the later higher years hostage and string out the settlement process. Accordingly, we agreed to a 75 percent discount for the years prior to 2007 but retained 100 percent for the years 2007 and after. We thought this was a great deal, and we were quite happy when the government agreed to it.

Our approach was very comprehensive, very technical, and very stressful. It was a stark contrast to the sloppiness exhibited by the law firms representing the other hospitals. At one point, the head of the consulting firm contacted DataGen asking if it would do the calculations for his groups, even though all the data and formulas for these calculations came from us. DataGen asked me what I thought and if they should cooperate with the request. I didn't hesitate to tell them "no." That meant the consulting firm's team had no option but to accept the government's settlement amounts, as they had no way to verify the accuracy of the government's numbers. We estimated that because those firms were unable to verify the government's numbers, these other hospital groups would receive payments that were reduced by between 1 and 3 percent.

# THE CONSULTING FIRM'S COLOSSAL—AND POTENTIALLY COSTLY—MISTAKE

There is one story that showcases the sloppiness of the individuals involved with the Indiana-based healthcare consulting firm, and it illuminates how this sloppiness could have led hospitals to lose out on hundreds of millions of dollars every year.

The story begins with the American Hospital Association (AHA), which represents nearly 5,000 hospitals, healthcare systems, healthcare networks, and other providers of care. In June 2011, it submitted a brief letter declaring that CMS should fix the payment rate in fiscal year 2012 to make up for the full amount of the agency's error. And in that letter, AHA asserted that hospitals were owed nearly $431 million. We were stunned. This was about 60 percent less than what the government owed the hospital industry. We knew we needed to meet with AHA to try to find out what led them to take this position.

We strategized at length about who should go to the meeting. The one person who we were certain to meet with was the author of the comment letter, a woman in her mid-thirties who worked in public policy. I was certain to attend, and we debated whether Dennis or Chris should as well. But in either scenario, that would make it two grumpy old men meeting with a young woman and the optics seemed bad to us. In the end, we decided that Steph and I would attend.

Our purpose was to determine how AHA came up with the $431 million figure. Near the conclusion of our meeting, which included another AHA official, we discussed the letter and asked if they had received any response from CMS to their letter. They said CMS wanted to know where AHA got the $431 million figure. We said we wondered about that as well. And when they asked me what I thought of the number, I responded that "it was low by a fair amount." I asked the public policy official who gave her the number, and she replied that it came from the head of the Indiana-based healthcare consulting firm.

Little did AHA know that in sending the letter and relying on the healthcare consulting firm for the amounts, it was shortchanging its members out of $600 million *per year, in perpetuity*. While we don't know what action (if any) AHA took after we met with them, we didn't hear them touting the $431 million figure again. Without that meeting, AHA members could have been severely shortchanged by CMS.

Steph and I determined that AHA and the head of the consulting firm did not know anything about the nature of the error or how to calculate it (AHA was relying on the consulting firm) and that there were clear risks for the hospitals affiliated with AHA (and the consulting firm) in their dealings with the government. However, we felt comfortable that our meeting got the AHA officials to understand that they needed to check with us before going too far out on any limb in the future.

In working through the settlement, the government required us to exchange with the other groups the list of hospitals and the years appealed to ensure there was no overlap. Unfortunately, we discovered that there were many duplicates, which occurred because the Indiana-based law firm had filed appeals on behalf of hospitals it wasn't representing and some of which *we* were representing—a haphazard and extremely reckless approach.

# DUPLICATE APPEALS AND DEALING WITH THE HOSPITALS

During the settlement process, each group that filed appeals had to present those appeals, broken down by hospital and by year, for to CMS to review. The predicate was for the three groups (the two law firms and us) to share with each other the providers and the years appealed.

Under the PRRB rules, each provider was to select a representative for each year appealed. Therefore, there should not have been duplicate appeals on any issue. But there were.

The issues predominantly involved the law firm and consulting firm based in Indiana. They had obtained representation letters for the hospitals that did not specify an issue or year. That firm also regularly filed appeals to piggyback on other cases. That meant they would have one representation letter for a hospital (in conflict with the PRRB rules), to file appeals on other issues. Given these prior practices, when the law firm started filing appeals related to the RF-BN issue, they either secured a representation letter that did not specify the year or issue at the beginning, or they relied on a letter they had secured previously related to another issue/appeal.

In comparing the list, we found many occasions where the Indiana law firm had filed appeals for hospitals in our groups. When we contacted those hospitals, they said they were unaware of these filings. Here's why this mattered: Duplicate appeals for the same issue, for the same year, were grounds for the PRRB to dismiss both appeals. This would leave the hospitals without an appeal and, depending on the timing, without a remedy to file another appeal.

We were learning all of this at the point in time when the hospitals could be expecting to receive money from the settlement. Instead, they could be facing the prospect of having their appeal dismissed. In most cases, the hospitals contacted the Indiana law firm, as did we, and instructed them to withdraw their appeal. Some of the hospitals had merged with other hospitals and then wanted to be in the law firm's appeal. We were happy to comply with their request, with one caveat: they needed to have all years (pre- and post-merger) we had appealed to the applicable law firm. This was done because we continued to look for ways to disadvantage the other groups. And if these hospitals became our clients, we did not want any conflicts of interest when representing them.

In some other instances, a hospital had been sold to a subsequent owner, who had signed an agreement with our firm. Yet the attorneys at the Indiana law firm just kept filing for the hospital, despite not having an agreement with the hospital to do so or for the payment of any fee. This clearly indicated that the law firm was not securing annual PRRB required certifications of common ownership. The fees in that firm's appeal were lower than our fees. But all the hospitals that we represented chose to stay with us: they were convinced we were the winners.

Until this point, we had tried to avoid talking with the other groups involved with this process. We always had our discussions with the Department of Justice, and then the others talked to DOJ separately. This generally worked well and was appropriate, given that we were the lead case and DOJ could not settle anything until we were in agreement. We had won the case, we had the court order in the *Cape Cod* case for the government to settle, all of our appeals were linked, and we had moved our cases to federal court in order to be under the legal umbrella of the order. In this sense, DOJ had to deal with us.

The government preferred not to deal with the law firms that represented the other groups, so it made an odd request: Would we, in effect, serve as the point of contact for them? We were unhappy about this request, as we didn't care for the other firms either (having already proven their incompetency in this case). But we recognized that our interest was in getting our clients paid as much as possible, as soon as possible, so we worked with the other firms—all while holding our noses.

Not surprisingly, the other firms greatly complicated our work, our lives, and even—potentially—our ability to reach a settlement with the government. They were pushy, which we could deal with, but their ignorance related to what we asked them to do proved to be a real challenge. They wanted to do their own thing, even if this meant they were doing the *wrong* thing. We had to persuade them not to pursue their own irresponsible ideas because they could have hurt us as well.

The government asked that we draft two versions of the agreement: one for the situation in which we provided the settlement amounts and one in which the government provided the amounts. This way, the agreements would be coordinated. Chris and Steph wrote both settlement agreements. Steph provided a governmental perspective, given her experience with these kinds of settlements from her time in government, and she reviewed the agreement to ensure it would pass muster with CMS. The latter document was the one the other groups eventually signed, and the former was the agreement we used.

The other law firm agreed to a few minor changes in the settlement language—the rough equivalent of typographical changes—so that the others could think they had provided input and could feel good about themselves. In reality, we had worked out everything with DOJ before the others were even brought into the process.

The government ultimately accepted our proposed terms with some modifications to the language contained in the official settlement. But before finalizing the agreement, they asked us to secure buy-in from the other groups and firms that were party to the settlement regarding the version of the agreement they would need to sign. The government had a diminished view of the other team—something that did not surprise me in the least—and did not want to deal with them.

All of this was a stressful process, given that we were the ones making the calculations on behalf of our clients, and there was always some possibility that one or more hospitals would disagree. Nevertheless, each hospital reviewed the calculations and ultimately agreed to their numbers. And with our cooperation secured, the DOJ agreed to our request that our hospitals be paid well in advance of any other hospitals in the settlement. But even with an accelerated pace, the government did not disburse the funds to the hospitals until one year after the court decision. That was par for the course, though, and ultimately beneficial.

# A HALF-BAKED THEORY ABOUT BOOSTING PRESIDENT OBAMA'S RE-ELECTION

One evening in April 2013, I attended a conference in Baltimore sponsored by the American Health Law Association. During a reception, I was chatting with Chris and one of his Akin Gump colleagues when we were approached by the head of the Indiana healthcare consulting firm. Chris immediately shot me a look that said, "What the hell does this asshole want?" I shared that sentiment, particularly after this individual started talking, and claimed that the settlement of our case had secured President Obama's November 2012 re-election. Our collective reply was, "What?"

He confidently told us that after the hospitals got paid in mid-2012, they used the money to hire more employees. And that, according to this individual, caused the unemployment rate to fall, which contributed to the Obama re-election (since a reduced unemployment would be a political positive for an incumbent president). I replied that the *real* reason the unemployment rate fell was that they stopped counting the folks who had stopped looking for work. He stuck to his theory but didn't stick around to debate it with us.

But the theory was clearly on his mind because the next day he approached Chris, who was in a large meeting room and about speak on a panel. This individual approached Chris and repeated the re-election theory, and then he stopped in his tracks and asked, "Is that microphone on?" Chris tapped the mic, which emitted a loud "thump, thump." Everyone had heard the half-baked theory. He immediately stopped talking and exited the room. But he wasn't finished.

The next day, I stepped out of a session to make a call, and when the session ended, this same individual exited the room and stood nearby waiting for me to finish my call. (I made several calls, as I was not anxious to talk to him.) When I finished, I started walking to an upstairs reception, at which point he started in on me again about the unemployment rate and the presidential election, insisting that the settlement was what got Obama re-elected. He rattled on for about a minute as we were walking, at which point I said to him, "Think about it. It's not logical that the hospitals caused the unemployment rate to drop." His assertion would have meant that the hospitals got paid in July/August 2012, and immediately hired so many new employees before September 2012 that they immediately reduced the national employment rate. The hospital industry seems "big" to those in the industry, but it's actually a very small portion of the economy. In addition, I pointed out that there is big-time data lag associated with the Bureau of Labor Statistics unemployment numbers, and told him, "You think that hospital spending just a few months before the November 2012 election caused the unemployment rate decrease. It's just not logical!" He kept carping at me as we were going up the escalator. When we reached the top, as were entering a large reception room, I turned to him and said, "Well, we know that no portion of the settlement monies for either of the two large publicly traded systems in your appeals caused this effect because they both had fraud take-backs, which negated the payments they were to receive." With that, he immediately shut up and walked away, as he knew that both of those entities were in his appeals.

# SUMMARY

- Even after winning the court case, we still needed to reach an agreement with the federal government on what our hospitals would be paid.

- The other firms involved with the case were playing by different rules and greatly complicated our work.

# 14

# THE FEDS PAY UP AND
# WE PAY OUT

The government agreed to pay our hospitals by the end of June
2012—months before the others—because we had agreed
to provide our payment amounts when the others could not. We
were preparing to invoice our clients as soon as the government
started sending them payments. In the meantime, however, we
had to set up the infrastructure needed to process large sums of
money and a large volume of transactions.

In mid-2011, we began the process of planning and setting
up the settlement processes. This included invoicing, banking,
collection, distribution of payments to the joint consultants and
attorneys, etc. We were working with a contractor to prepare the
invoices, which we standardized to make them as simple as possible. Next, we worked to ensure that the emails and addressees
were current, which was a critical element, since virtually all
contact with the hospitals was by email.

The plan was to have the hospitals electronically transfer
monies into an account that we would establish for that purpose.
(We had initially asked the government if the funds could be

transferred to Akin Gump, and then have them make the distributions to the hospitals, but that idea was rejected). Once the account was created, we wanted it to be secure, given the ever-present risk of bank failure, but also isolated from other bank monies. The first large money center bank I contacted never followed up after our first conversation. The next bank proposed that we set up a trust, but we could not come to terms on how the trust should be structured. I ultimately talked to a regional bank, M&T Bank, which is based in Buffalo but operated in Maryland, as well as six other states and Washington, D.C. We worked with them to set up what was, in effect, a checking account without checks. We had transfers coming in and transfers going out to our joint consultants or partners, with the remainder of each being transferred to a separate trust/investment account in my name. Accordingly, the main corporate account was always to be at or near zero. There were funds coming in each day from the hospitals and funds going out at least every week. What I wanted to avoid was being paid all the money from the hospitals but then having something go wrong with the bank and being liable to the joint consultants/partners, let alone the IRS and the state tax collector.

The account we established was a non-interest-bearing checking account. We could do this and be safe from liability because the recently enacted Dodd-Frank Act provided that any non-interest-bearing account would receive federal government protection without any limitation up until December 31, 2012. (M&T was the only bank that pointed out this regulation, which confirmed we were right to choose them.) Since we expected most of the funds to have been in and then out of this account, any residue would be very minimal by that date. (We were also working on tax and estate planning for myself. For investment management services, we talked to three different firms and settled on Wilmington Trust, which was the trust subsidiary of M&T Bank.)

Simultaneously, we were working with the government to attempt to pinpoint the timing of the payment to the hospitals. We wanted to invoice the hospitals immediately after they received the payment from the government, to minimize the risk that they would spend to money before sending us our share. The deadline we verbally agreed to with the government was June 30, 2012. Much to our surprise, the government said it would pay our hospitals *earlier* than the original agreed-upon date. In fact, the date kept moving forward, and we started hearing from hospitals as early as the first week of May that the federal government had sent them the funds by electronic transfer. While each hospital received a different amount, the largest sum was about $30 million. The regional director of one hospital wrote to us afterwards to express his gratitude for what we had recovered:

> *I want to personally thank you, Chris, Stephanie, and all those behind the scenes for making this happen. I appreciate keeping me updated on the appeal's progression. I applaud your approach of maintaining a low profile until the funds are actually received. While I understand the rationale of the other firms and for-profit providers for announcing early, I believe yours was the correct course.*

# KRISTINA

When the appeal process started, my oldest daughter, Kristina, was studying engineering at Elizabethtown College in Pennsylvania. In early 2008, she finished up her coursework and returned home. She was figuring out employment options when we learned that Jayne's cancer had returned, and she wanted to be near her mom but also keep busy. With Jayne no longer in a position to be deeply involved in the appeal process, Kristina took over the critical—but sometimes mind-numbing—work. Jayne would be next to her, lying on a couch. This revived a routine from a few years earlier when she would sit with Kristina and help with her high school homework.

The appeal filings were in full swing. We were also litigating the appeal in the D.C. District Court and needed to continue to file for rate-year appeals going forward and for the various Notice of Program Reimbursement years prior to fiscal year 2007. These filings entailed very detailed and precise filings, and meeting various requirements set out by the Provider Reimbursement Review Board. Having studied engineering, Kristina had the aptitude and background we needed to ensure that all the appeal documents were assembled correctly that were eventually filed by the attorneys.

This was no small task. About 730 hospitals had joined our litigation, and an appeal needed to be filed for each one, and for each year. And the process continued through 2009, 2010, and 2011. She mastered the intricacies of the filing/documentation process and made no mistakes. She knew, as we all did, that any error could have been the basis for prejudicing any hospital's claim for payment.

When the court ruled in our favor in early 2011, another highly complex process got underway. It involved reconciling hospitals in our groups and those represented by our competitors. The government required this reconciliation to avoid any duplicate payments among the hospital years under appeal in any resultant settlement. There was also the matter of the work involved with moving all our groups/hospitals to federal court, which kept the pressure on the government to settle—they wanted to delay payment as long as possible. The other groups had filed appeals on behalf of any hospital they believed was entitled to appeal— regardless of whether the hospital had signed on with that group. That meant we had to identify the respective hospitals and then coordinate with the other group to have them remove that hospital from their filings. We also had to communicate and coordinate with the hospitals themselves—a very laborious and time-consuming process, with no margin for error. This effort was spearheaded by Kristina, and she did an outstanding job.

Our next big challenge was making sure we got paid by the hospitals once they had received their funds from the government, as part of the settlement. This meant ensuring the amount included on each of the hundreds of invoices was correct, and then completing the painstaking process of confirming the accuracy of each hospital's contact information (there was typically a single person who needed to be reached).

The process also involved tracking which hospitals had paid, and then following up with those that had not. Also, we were transferring the appropriate portions of the settlement for our partners, per the related agreements. It was a tribute to Kristina's efforts that the vast majority of the payments came in promptly— and that we collected 99.2 percent of the funds we were owed (the shortfall primarily involved hospitals that had closed or declared bankruptcy).

Kristina and I both have strong personalities and a strong work ethic. We both work hard and long and expect others to do the same. As an illustration, after the appeal had been settled, I was working in the foundation I had established with some of the funds collected from the hospitals, running my consulting practices, and developing a professional racing program. Someone asked one of my friends why I was still working so hard, and he replied, "Look at it this way: Before, Ted spent 100 percent of his time in consulting, another 100 percent of his time on the appeal and the other 100 percent of his time in racing. Now that the appeal is resolved, he has 100 percent of his time free for other projects."

Kristina has the same type of work ethic, so it was inevitable that we occasionally butted heads. But it was all in service of reaching the same goal, and as we worked through our occasional differences, we grew closer. Given that a glitch at any point could have cost us time, credibility, and capital, I wouldn't have wanted anyone else in her role. She made everything run smoothly and did so with a quiet persistence that everyone on the team admired—no one more so than me.

The process of disbursing the proceeds was tedious, but it ultimately went off without a hitch. By agreement, the first 10 percent of what we received from the hospitals went to DataGen or the Healthcare Association of New York State (HANYS), depending on the agreement and the hospitals. Of the remaining 90 percent, 10 percent went to the attorneys. From the remaining portion, Ron—the initial funder of the effort—received about 18 percent, and then the consultants were paid 25 percent of the funds we received from the hospitals they had brought to us. After everyone else was paid, my share was about 50 percent. In addition to my share of the risk-based fee, I was also paid a separate fixed fee for every hospital in the appeal.

There was one other detail: while the funds came from the government, they were taxable income. I don't know how everyone else treated this income, but I paid the top rate to both the feds and the state of Maryland. The last thing I wanted was to be chased by some government bureaucrat for more money in the future. I needed to turn this page of my life and move forward.

I felt relieved that the process was nearing completion, but I was still anxious, as we weren't in the end zone yet. I was still engaged in finding firms that could help me with tax planning and estate planning, deciding on investment managers, developing a variety of trusts, and preparing for what I might do next. Also, I knew that as I worked through these processes, I was making decisions that were going to affect me and my daughters for the rest of our lives. Yes, I was happy to have succeeded. But I was reflective about my future, and that of my family and friends. With so much happening, and so much to think about, there was no time for a victory party or jubilation.

## SUMMARY

- The federal government agreed to pay our hospitals by the end of June 2012, but we started hearing from the hospitals as early as the first week of May that the government was sending them funds by electronic transfer. We were worried that the hospitals would spend the money quickly and then claim they were unable to pay us.

- By the end of 2012, we had collected 99.2 percent of what we were owed—with virtually all of the unpaid funds attributed to eleven hospitals that had declared bankruptcy.

# 15

# JAYNE

As I mentioned at the outset of this book, my wife, Jayne, fought a battle with breast cancer during a three-year period that overlapped with much of the appeal story recounted in this book. I have included the story of her battle because she had an integral role in the appeal and worked on it alongside me from the beginning. She developed personal relationships with the attorneys, as well as our hospital clients, worked with me on the appeals documentation, and assisted greatly in filing the annual appeal documents. Throughout the process, Jayne and I were always discussing strategy. She provided moral support, and I thought of her—as did everyone else—as my alter ego.

I met Jayne in 1978. We were working at the same hospital, Baltimore County General (she was a clinical dietitian in acute care), and her boss had suggested I ask her out. I didn't, as I had some concerns about being involved with someone who also worked at the hospital. When her boss learned that I was planning to leave the hospital for a new job, he reiterated the suggestion. So, I did ask her out—on the afternoon of my last day. I asked if she had weekend plans, and she didn't, so we went out the next night.

We went to dinner and spent time together. After many such dates, we became closer. I visited her family in California, and she visited mine in Maryland. Not long after our first date, we started living together. Jayne was renting a room from a lady near the hospital, and I was living alone, so living together made economic sense. Amid some adversity that we both experienced in our professional lives, we supported one another in ways that made us realize we belonged together.

I ultimately took a position in Cumberland, Maryland, as the CFO of a health system, and Jayne moved there with me, leaving her job in Baltimore behind. She quickly found work in Cumberland, a geographically isolated town of about 20,000 people. This isolation helped us to become even closer. It was there we decided to get married. We held the wedding on February 4, 1984, and it was conducted by a friend, Ralph Ciampa, who was the chaplain at the hospital. Ralph said it was the only wedding where the entire congregation could be in the wedding picture. Twelve people attended, mostly friends from both sides.

In late 1984, we relocated to Highland, Maryland, because I had taken a job in Washington. Our first daughter, Kristina, was born later that year, and our second daughter, Allie, was born in 1988. Jayne scaled back her work schedule considerably while our girls were young, and then resumed her dietitian work once they were in school, primarily with the Little Sisters of the Poor.

One of our favorite places to go was Deep Creek Lake, about two-and-a-half hours away, in western Maryland. We bought a house there in 1993, and we would go there many weekends each year. Jayne loved it and had a well-developed social network there.

In 2001, a mammogram revealed a small lump in Jayne's left breast. She had been quite vigilant about her annual checkups, going to the gynecologist and having a breast examination and mammogram every year. Once the lump was discovered, the doctors recommended surgery. The American College of Surgeons' protocol at the time was to have a lumpectomy performed and then have the tumor biopsied. She did that, and once the doctors knew the tumor was malignant, they also removed all the lymph nodes on her left side and biopsied them all (they found no trace of cancer in any of them). Because of the small size of the lump (Jayne's surgeon told us it was the smallest tumor he had ever removed from a breast) and finding no traces in the lymph nodes, they prescribed radiation at the tumor site. No chemotherapy was recommended.

For the next seven years, Jayne continued her annual checkup routine of seeing her oncologist and surgeon and getting breast examinations and mammograms. She was also taking an oral medication, Tamoxifin, which is a prophylactic for the cancer spreading. When we weren't going to Deep Creek Lake, we would often go to Myrtle Beach, South Carolina. Jayne loved it, and in late 2007 we almost bought a house there. It's good we didn't because it was also about this time that Jayne began to mention to her doctors that she was having a pain in her left hip. They dismissed it as being caused by arthritis. On February 21, 2008, Jayne and I, and our daughters, Kristina and Allie, were at a restaurant celebrating Allie's birthday. After leaving the restaurant, Jayne tried to get into our car, but immediately complained of extreme pain in her left hip. We got her into the car and took her home. She took some over-the-counter pain medication, but the excruciating pain persisted, and she struggled to sleep. We all figured it was the arthritic pain and that it would be better the next day. It wasn't.

We took her to the emergency room at a local hospital the

following day. They examined her, gave her pain medicine, and decided to do an MRI on her left hip. It revealed a large tumor, which they believed was a byproduct of the breast cancer. We were told that breast cancer cells like to metastasize to bones. At that time, they told us she may have only months to live and would never walk again—news that left all of us in complete horror, shock, and disbelief.

Jayne had done everything to the "t" as prescribed by her doctors and more, while also maintaining a healthy diet and routine exercise regimen. How could it not have rung a bell with her oncologist, general practitioner, surgeon, and so on, that she was suffering from hip pain in only one hip for months and months? Particularly when the hip is one of the most common places breast cancer would metastasize? What went wrong? Was there a mistake? None of it made sense.

She stayed overnight at that hospital, with me by her side. The following day, she was transferred to the hospital where she had been treated previously for her cancer. She was then seen by an orthopedic surgeon, who concluded that the tumor was inoperable, since the bone was brittle and there was a risk of cancer cells being released if they penetrated the bone structure. The oncologist concluded that since the cancer was contained within the bone, radiation was the better option, to be followed by chemotherapy, so she started radiation treatment. During this time, my friend Graham was researching the cancer diagnosis, treatment options, and related issues while I was exploring the side effects of her treatment.

The oncologist recommended that Jayne participate in a clinical trial (we now understand this was not a good sign). There were tests being conducted of a new oral drug called Sutent, and the results were going to be compared to what was the benchmark, Avastin. She was randomly assigned to Sutent, which we wanted. After several months of the trial, she experienced severe abdominal pain and bowel-related issues. She was subsequently dropped from the trial and began traditional chemotherapy on a drug called Taxol. She was also given a bone-strengthening drug. This course of chemotherapy concluded in 2009; she had continued her routine checkups throughout this entire period. Jayne was always worried about "the cell that got away," since her very first diagnosis in 2001. Her fear—and ours—was realized in February 2008. The doctors did not know what we know now about cancer: how it spreads, dormancy, etc. The clinicians made decisions and recommendations based on their knowledge and their interpretations of that knowledge. Oncologists are trying to be positive when talking to patients and can often skirt the reality of the situation. As a result, patients may not know the true situation.

We stopped going to Deep Creek Lake, as it was often difficult for Jayne to leave the house. Early in 2010, she resumed chemotherapy. This was not a good sign but viewed as necessary for her stage of cancer and its progression. This process involved taking her to chemo once per week, which were not as intense as her previous rounds of chemo.

In early November 2010, Jayne was sightseeing with a friend in Washington, D.C., when she tripped and bumped her head on a museum step. She was taken to the hospital and given a CT scan, which revealed brain metastasis.

A few days later, on November 8, Jayne started radiation to treat her brain metastasis. This was also the day of oral arguments at the Court of Appeals. She insisted that I go to the court with the lawyers rather than with her. Kristina went with her instead.

The radiation treatment was then followed by another round of chemotherapy.

On Christmas Day, 2010, she started talking in ways we couldn't understand. We didn't know what to make of this, so a few days later we took her to the hospital for her scheduled chemo visit, which happened to be my birthday. The doctors told us that during her most recent blood draw, a week prior, her liver enzymes were off. This was a sign that the cancer had spread to the liver—something we hadn't been told was an issue—and that now her liver enzymes were in even worse condition. This explained why Jayne was talking gibberish. The doctors told my daughters and I that she only had a few days to live. I had always applied the same tenacity toward Jayne's treatment, and my view of her cancer, as I had applied to the appeal: *never give up*. In a game of draw poker, I would keep drawing three cards until the other players fell asleep. This approach was not working now. When talking to our children, Jayne and I always referred to one another as "mommy" and "daddy." In late 2010, Jayne started saying to our kids, "Daddy's got to let me go." This was a telling sign that she had had enough of her treatment. It may have also been a signal that she knew the end was nearing and was comfortable with that but needed to get our kids and me comfortable too.

In the evening of December 28, 2010, Jayne and my daughters sang me Happy Birthday in the hospital room. After the last words in the song "Happy Birthday to You," Jayne added, "You look like a monkey, and smell like one too."

After December 28, Jayne was in what was called "comfort care"—she was beginning to pass. Because this was going to happen so rapidly, the hospital staff said they would not transfer her to hospice (which was the normal protocol). Instead, they allowed us to use the adjoining room so we could stay nearby.

The following day, the four of us (Jayne, Kristina, Allie, and myself) were in Jayne's hospital room. Jokingly, Jayne said, "I want a cigarette," even though she never smoked. This was a sign she was losing her mental comprehension, which was another stage of passing. People sent flowers to her room, and she would say to us, "Take them away, take them away." We believe she saw this as a sign the end was near, and it was coming too soon.

In the days after December 28, I had to make a plan for Jayne's passing. I knew there would be a memorial service, so I called my friend Terry and told him the news about Jayne. I asked him to find Ralph Ciampa, who was the chaplain who had married Jayne and me in 1984. Terry tracked down Ralph at the University of Pennsylvania in Philadelphia, where he was the chaplain.

While I was trying to focus on Jayne, my mind was full of things that needed to be done. On December 30, I had planned to meet with someone at a funeral home, which was a short drive from the hospital. As I was preparing to leave, Jayne's psychologist said to me, "Frequently, in times of stress, we think of things to do that only serve to keep us from doing the things we should do." I elected to stay with Jayne.

Since we were all there together, the girls searched the internet and started playing songs that we knew were Jayne's favorites. These included "Pink Cadillac" by Bruce Springsteen, "Brown Eyed Girl" by Van Morrison, "Parallel Universe" by the Red Hot Chili Peppers, "Wild World" by Cat Stevens, and "California Dreamin'" by The Mamas and The Papas. Although she could not speak at this point, she smiled upon hearing the songs. This went on for several hours. Even though Jayne was in sort of a comatose state, she could still hear. Had I left, I would have missed this very special moment.

From that point on, we were all hesitant to leave Jayne's side, but my daughters had realized Jayne was not wearing her wedding band (she had trouble wearing rings due to swelling in her fingers from the various drugs she was taking), and it was important to them that when she passed she was wearing it. With Carol, one of Jayne's best friends, by her side, as well as me, my daughters raced home to pick up the band so I could place it on her finger for the last time.

Allie and Kristina stayed awake to monitor Jayne's breathing that night and into the early hours of the next morning, while I rested in the hospital bed in the adjoining room. At about 2:00 a.m., Allie went downstairs to take a break from the heaviness of the situation and had a long conversation with a gentleman in the lobby. This left Kristina and Jayne, who had an unspeakable bond with each other, alone for quite some time. During this time, Kristina told her,

*I love you, Mommy. We all love you with everything we have. I promise you that for the rest of our lives, Dad, Allie, and me will take care of each other, and we will carry you with us in our hearts forever. It's okay to go now, mommy, it's okay to go. Pop [Jayne's father] is waiting for you.*

Shortly thereafter, Allie came back to the room and immediately noticed a dramatic difference in Jayne's breathing patterns—slow and shallow. They called the nurse and woke me up.

Allie and Kristina had been talking to Jayne. They knew she couldn't respond but were confident she could hear them. When I entered the room, they said, "Dad's here." With us all by her side, Jayne passed at 2:55 a.m., on New Year's Eve. It was almost as if she was waiting for the three of us to be there together before passing.

The three of us were stunned by what had just happened. It was like, "Is she really gone?" After the nurses and doctor left, the three of us remained there with Jayne for about forty-five minutes, alone. We all felt like saying to her, "Jayne, you can't leave now, the story's not over yet." But she was gone.

The girls eventually said, "What do we do now?"

I said, "We go home."

"And leave her here alone?" they asked.

This is what our family was like. It was the hardest thing any of us has ever had to do. It was now just the three of us—not four.

There are a lot of painful memories every year on Allie's birthday, my birthday, Christmas, and New Year's Eve. Hopefully, time will heal the pain, but it hasn't yet.

Two weeks after Jayne's death, the Court of Appeals ruled in our favor. In talking about the decision with a friend of mine, I mentioned Jayne. He said, "She knew before we knew." I believe he was right. After the oral argument, I had called Jayne to tell her about the proceedings. She went outside and talked to Kristina, who was walking along our long driveway. Jayne was crying and told Kristina, "We won. The decision was two of three in our favor. Don't ever let the money change you. Always stay true to who you are." Even though the decision ultimately was all three in our favor, Jayne knew then that we were going to prevail.

I still think of Jayne regularly and treasure the memory of our time together. The best expression of our relationship is contained in a book of poems called *The Prophet*, by Kahlil Gibran. Jayne included portions of one of those poems in the marriage vows she wrote for us.

*You were born together, and together you shall be forever-*
*more.*
*You shall be together when the white wings of death scatter*
*your days.*
*Ay, you shall be together even in the silent memory of God.*
*But let there be spaces in your togetherness,*
*And let the winds of the heavens dance between you.*

*Love one another, but make not a bond of love:*
*Let it rather be a moving sea between the shores of your*
*souls.*
*Fill each other's cup but drink not from one cup.*
*Give one another of your bread but eat not from the same*
*loaf.*
*Sing and dance together and be joyous, but let each one of*
*you be alone,*
*Even as the strings of a lute are alone though they quiver with*
*the same music.*

*Give your hearts, but not into each other's keeping.*
*For only the hand of Life can contain your hearts.*
*And stand together yet not too near together: For the pillars*
*of the temple stand apart,*
*And the oak tree and the cypress grow not in each other's*
*shadow.*

# A CELEBRATION OF JAYNE'S LIFE

Shortly after Jayne passed, we began planning a celebration of Jayne's life. We decided that this celebration would not be a somber memorial service, but rather an event that would reflect Jayne's fun-loving persona—a "celebration" in the truest sense of the word. It was held on January 19, at an interfaith center in Columbia, Maryland, which is not far from our home. We decided to have it in the late afternoon, to allow more folks to attend after work.

Jayne was an integral part of my business, which meant that many of our business contacts knew her and elected to attend. This included the attorneys in our appeal and many folks I had worked with over the years. Jayne had spent many years as a consulting dietitian in a long-term care facility, and many folks from that arena attended too. She had many other friends attend as well, from as far away as California. In the end, there were about 150 people present.

Ralph Ciampa (the individual who married Jayne and I) presided over the celebration, and we asked three of Jayne's friends to speak: Libby Pope, a childhood friend, who talked about some of the funny things they did as hippies in the San Francisco area; Carol Lombardo, a friend since their college years; and Linda Reger, a colleague of Jayne's at the Little Sisters of the Poor Nursing Home, who talked about what Jayne meant to her and how she helped her.

I also spoke, as did Kristina and Allie. Kristina spoke of the deep and unique bond that she had with Jayne, as well as Jayne's genuine, pure, and real love. She described how when Jayne loved, she did so with her whole heart—without judgment and without expecting anything in return. She would make any sacrifice if it meant she could help someone. Allie emphasized that Jayne was a constant advocate for her and that she was grateful to have her as a mom. She also described how Jayne touched many people and was "one of a kind."

I wrestled with how I could synthesize, in brief comments, the relationship Jayne and I had, and all that she meant to me. I spoke about "who" Jayne was and that she unknowingly influenced how I lived and who I had become. I described her as my best friend, lover, wife, companion, advisor, confidant, supporter, cheerleader, business associate/partner, alter ego, kindred spirit, and much more. I pointed out that, "She created an environment for me to fulfill dreams that I might not have otherwise experienced. Do it, and do it now, don't wait—this was Jayne. And, this is how we were." I concluded by quoting an email sent to me on the day of the celebration from a friend of more than thirty years. "Jayne was a warm, caring, and loving lady—you were a lucky man to have someone in your life that good." Indeed, I was.

Before concluding, Ralph read our marriage vows—the way we started. After the presentations and comments, those who were there and did not know Jayne had a good sense of what she was like and how she lived.

Before the celebration and during the reception, we projected pictures of Jayne through the various phases of her life: early childhood, high school and college, young adulthood (pre-me), our life as a couple, and her life with us as a family. My daughters also compiled a music playlist for the slide show. Before the cancer diagnosis, Jayne and Kristina would spend summer weekends at our house at Deep Creek Lake, and the two-and-a-half hour drives to and from Deep Creek were always accompanied by the music of the Red Hot Chili Peppers on endless loop. During these drives, Jayne would jokingly tell Kristina, "At my memorial you must play the Red Hot Chili Peppers." And that we did, supplemented by her other favorite bands and songs. By the time the celebration ended, everyone could understand and appreciate what made Jayne special. This was precisely as we had planned it—we wanted folks to have a complete picture of the remarkable life she had lived.

As the event wrapped up, one of my friends said to me, "This was the most uplifting experience I have had and should be in the dictionary under Celebration of Life."

And it was.

# 16

# CREATING A FOUNDATION

In early 2012, I began to realize that we were going to get money from the settlement. Also, because of our estimates, I had a sense of what I would get. A notion I had in late 2011 came to me again: the idea of starting a foundation. This concept started to percolate in mid-2012, and I began formulating a plan. The foundation would focus on both health and policy and would fund unbiased research. Today, the foundation seeks to improve healthcare for patients and their families. We highlight emerging issues and foster public discussion around healthcare and health policy.

I solicited Graham's agreement to work with me in the foundation. In September 2012, we began developing the legal documents to create the foundation and formally applied to the IRS for tax exemption. We were told approval would come but that it would take ten months. In fact, it came in ten weeks.

The early approval caught us by surprise, so we immediately turned to the policy dimension. To date, we have conducted or sponsored the following research:

- The provision of charity care by not-for-profit hospitals and the benefit local communities receive from this care relative to the benefit these hospitals receive from their tax exemption.
- A review of the Washington, D.C. healthcare market after health reform.
- A study with the American Public Health Association to identify issues in public health related to health reform.

Other activities have included:

- Awarding dissertation support grants to support doctoral candidates.
- Funding intramural fellowships at the National Institutes of Health (NIH).
- Conducting a series of policy briefings at a major policy-oriented university.
- Supporting a series of trade press briefings.
- Developing research projects, such as one on patient engagement to identify the best ways to communicate health plan price and quality via websites to patients with varying degrees of literacy and numeracy.
- Evaluating quality measures assigned to public and private sector health plans and providers. There are several different measures, they vary widely, and they're extremely difficult for patients and providers to understand. In relation to these quality measures, we reviewed and examined the "weighting" of quality measures into a combined score to be used when assessing the effectiveness of health plans and providers and how accurately this weighting reflects patient preferences.

- Promoting collaborations in research among the mathematical modeling and biological disciplines to identify better research paths. This project was in partnership with the National Cancer Institute (NCI) and the Breast Cancer Research Foundation.

In mid-2014, I became concerned that the foundation had been over-emphasizing public policy, so we sought to identify research topics in the health space. As a result, since late 2014, the foundation has been very active in the cancer research area. We have funded several large research projects, with more planned.

One project, at Johns Hopkins University, involves the use of nanoparticles in the treatment of breast cancer via hyperthermia to see if the nanoparticles can track down metastatic cells, and whether nanoparticles can have an impact on stimulating an immune response to breast cancer. (Very few women die these days from the main/initial site breast cancer; it's the metastatic sites that get them.)

Another project is at the Wistar Institute, a biomedical research outfit in Philadelphia. It involved three different, but related, areas of investigation into breast cancer: metastasis, cell dormancy, and reemergence. There was also a follow-on project focused on brain metastasis. We hope to find out the communication linkages between main breast cancer sites and metastatic sites, why breast cancer cells go dormant, how/why they remain that way, and why they reemerge later (often more aggressively). By exploring these three dimensions, we hope to find out how these processes work and what we can do to change things.

We are also working with NIH and the NCI on several fronts for programmatic work, and we have funded research fellowships at NIH.

My profession today is automobile racing, and I see some important parallels between racing and the work of the foundation. In racing, you are constantly evaluating and tweaking to be better. Complacency is dangerous—it is how you get hurt. That's the connection to healthcare, where key questions include, "How does this treatment or policy decision impact patients?" "Why do we approach treatment that way?" and "Should Medicare ignore socio-economic factors in making payments?" These issues are urgent, because, every day, thousands of patients are experiencing a healthcare system that can—and should—do better.

So, why do we do this? Below is an unsolicited email the Wistar Institute received in response to the press release announcing our creation of The Jayne Koskinas Ted Giovanis Breast Cancer Research Consortium:

*Hello,*

*I just wanted to take a moment to thank you for establishing The Jayne Koskinas Ted Giovanis Breast Cancer Research Consortium at your institute. On April 2, 2014, at age 36, I was diagnosed with Stage IV invasive ductal carcinoma (ER+/PR+, HER2-) with metastases in my liver, lungs, adrenal gland, spleen, and many bones. Thankfully, I have experienced a tremendous response to traditional therapies (Taxol chemotherapy for 16 weeks, monthly Zometa, and now a combination of Arimidex and Faslodex), but I know the harsh reality that Stage IV is incurable and the median life expectancy is just 3 years. I have so much more to give to this world than three years would allow. With targeted therapies and immuno-oncology, more treatments that can extend my life are just on the horizon, but they won't happen without basic cancer research. Thank you so much for recognizing the need for research specific to metastatic breast cancer. You are giving women like me hope for a future. Many thanks and best of luck on your research.*

*Jennifer*

We do what we do on behalf of the Jaynes and the Jennifers of the world. We know that the likelihood is that things won't change fast, but our work provides real hope for those we are still able to save.

# CONCLUSION

L ong after the appeal was over and settled, I began reflecting on our journey. While there was nothing easy about it, I always knew it was the right thing to do. The government had made an error, which had led hospitals to lose out on billions of dollars. They deserved the money—federal law required it—and the government needed to be held accountable.

But there was one dimension of the journey that I had not considered at the outset. It was brought home to me during a conversation with Steph. She said that few people would think to sue the federal government, and even fewer would pursue the case as long or as vigorously as I did. I could understand that. But what she said next was particularly memorable: "The reason most people would not want to sue the government was that they feared retaliation."

I had never thought about this, but I knew from experience that the so-called "Deep State" exists. To me, the term refers to federal government employees whose jobs are all but guaranteed and their employment is not tied to any candidate or party (in Washington shorthand, they are known as "career" bureaucrats). As a result, they are insulated from the normal employment influences of their superiors and while they tend to be liberal, their goal is self-preservation. And as I said at the start of the book, they are ostensibly nonpolitical, but they can—and will—use the full force of the federal government to manipulate public policy and to defend their interests, whether those interests are ideological or personal (or both).

I also knew that the government wields extraordinary—often unlimited—power. Government officials can retaliate against individuals and institutions in a variety of ways. They have the power to work across departments and exercise their power against you. (An example would be to allege that you've failed to comply with a law or regulation.) This could involve departments like transportation, environment, energy, and, of course, the Internal Revenue Service. Imagine having your tax returns audited into oblivion. Responding to such harassment—and perhaps even fighting it—would be very time-consuming, very expensive, and very stressful. It's not surprising that most people capitulate when the government comes after them.

When we were first looking for hospitals to be the lead plaintiffs, I was surprised that we had to lean on them to come forward. They were afraid that CMS would retaliate against them, which is a sad statement about the way in which people feel threatened by their own government. We had to convince the hospitals that being out front was safest, as any government retaliation would be crystal clear.

At that time, I did not think to wonder whether I was at risk from government retaliation. I might have been, but even if I thought so at the time, I doubt I would have done things any differently. When I believe I'm doing the right thing, I will not back down. I once resigned from a job after six weeks (leaving me unemployed) because I believed my employer—the owner of a hospital—was a crook. I feared that my association with the hospital owner would taint me, and I also knew that resigning was the ethical thing to do. Similarly, I once told a boss that one of my subordinates deserved a $5,000 performance raise and he was going to get it even if the money would have to come for my pay. (He got the raise.)

## THE FOUR PERSONALITIES OF TED GIOVANIS

I once described myself to the attorneys as a combination of four different personalities: "I have the attributes of Bruce Willis in *Die Hard* the coolness and calmness of Robert Duvall in *Apocalypse Now*, the cunning of Anthony Hopkins in *Silence of the Lambs*, and the craziness of Jack Nicholson in *The Shining.*" One of my attorneys asked, "How do we know which personality is the dominant one at any given time?" I responded, "You don't."

While my mindset throughout the appeal was one of being "beyond fear," I've also known that one is always a potential target. Until writing this book, I've been extremely discrete in my discussions about winning the appeal and securing a large financial settlement from the government. It only takes one bureaucrat—and not even a senior one—to decide to start poking around and your entire existence can be turned upside down. Even with my discretion, the thought has crossed my mind that it might not have been coincidence that I have had my taxes audited multiple times in recent years.

The power of government was one of the many lessons I

learned throughout the appeal process. There were several others.

*Lawyers who represent you can be your greatest allies, but they also have the potential to make your life miserable.* There was a point in the process when we were in discussions with the three appeal groups—composed of our team and the two law firms. We butted heads with the two firms throughout the appeal, and it became necessary to find out what the others were doing. We were in the strongest position to do this, but the two law firms kept threatening and trying to do things with the government behind our backs. While this may not have been wise, it was their right. They kept telling us they wanted to work with us, so long as we did what they wanted. Fat chance. We always did what we believed was best for our clients. If that involved working with the others, then fine. If not, then we did our own thing.

At one point, we needed to discover what the California-based law firm was doing. They kept saying they were going to do something, but we needed to know if they'd really done it. Dennis, one attorney on our team, had a relationship with the lead attorney at the California firm on the RF-BN issue, so we had him make the contact and try to determine what the California firm really was doing. He reported back that the firm was doing nothing. But then he told us that he talked to his contact for more than an hour. I asked him why, because I knew from experience that the longer he talked, the greater the risk that he would convey to his contact what *we* were doing. I told Dennis that we weren't in the minor league, where the players can be chatty with one another. This was the major league and both sides were playing hardball. I told him that once he found the answer we needed, the conversation should have ended. He responded by yelling at me: "I can't work like this!" He then stormed out of the room.

I looked at Chris and Steph and told them, "From now on, tell him no more than he needs to know to do what we want him to do." They agreed—and from that point forward we never told him much of anything that could be of value to the others. This was a little complicated, given that our primary legal agreement for attorney representation was with Dennis's firm. But we made it work.

This episode coincided with another issue we had with an attorney. During the settlement process, we started dealing with the duplicate appeals of the other firms and sales of hospitals in our appeals. In reviewing PRRB documents provided by the hospitals, we discovered that a Houston-based partner at the law firm where Dennis worked was representing a consulting firm that was working for other hospitals in filing RF-BN PRRB appeals. We also discovered this firm was writing newsletters and touting its RF-BN qualifications, and it appeared that they were trying to solicit other RF-BN clients for themselves.

In my judgment, this was a clear conflict of interest, and in violation of our agreement with the firm, which specified that it would not solicit or accept clients who were involved with the pending rural-floor issue. The conflict took us by surprise, but large, diversified law firms like this one often discover that they have conflicts between their different practice groups. In this case, while the firm should have detected in advance that there was a conflict, they told us they were not aware of it, which we believed. We called on the firm to have the attorney withdraw from the engagement. The firm's general counsel and our counsel then spent an inordinate amount of time trying to resolve the issue. The answer was simple: the partner should drop the other client. The firm would not admit they were wrong and risk having us sue them or, even worse, not pay them. But they ultimately ceased the solicitations and kept quiet—as far as we know—which was our principal objective.

*When you're suing the federal government, assume it will be more difficult to win than you think. Win or lose, it will take a very long time.* The agencies of the federal government, such as the Department of Health and Human Services, will go to great lengths and often resort to underhanded tactics to avoid admitting an error. The Department of Justice claimed that our case should be dismissed because I had improperly submitted the initial comment letter, and their argument rested on a tendentious definition of the word "please" (an argument Judge Lamberth dismissed). Similarly, the government claimed never to have received my comment letter—even though a CMS employee signed a receipt acknowledging of the letter's receipt. Even so, we lost in the District Court, thanks to a DOJ claim that wasn't supported by the facts. And it bears repeating that nearly six years elapsed between my initial email exchange with CMS and when the government started paying the hospitals. In our case, I suspect Mike of CMS was driving the government's resistance and slowing down the proceedings. He wasn't going to concede anything until he'd moved out of the Division of Acute Care where he'd been working. And coincidence or not, the issue didn't get resolved until he had moved to another division.

*Be prepared for many different scenarios—and adapt to the unexpected.* There were several parallels between the appeal and the endurance races I drive in. As former Secretary of Defense Donald Rumsfeld once put it, there are "known knowns," "known unknowns," "unknown knowns," and "unknown unknowns." While you can do a lot of planning for the "knowns," it's the "unknowns" that ultimately matter more. In an endurance race, for example, it's guaranteed that drivers will need to switch off, tires will need to changed, and that the car will need to be refueled. But with a long race, there is also a complex matrix of decisions to make. There can be electrical failures, wire failures, and—given the duration of the race—human failures. With part of the race being contested at night, there's also a greater likelihood of being affected by the mistakes of other drivers. There can also be weather issues. If it rains, will the windshield wipers work the entire time? Will the windshield defogger work? It's all a matter of being prepared for the unexpected—and having the agility to pivot on extremely short notice. Indeed, the strength of your team is measured by how well they adapt to change and adversity.

With the appeal, we tried to anticipate everything, and we spent a huge amount of time planning for a variety of different scenarios—thinking through how one action or another might affect the many different parties involved with this issue. I'd estimate that 80 percent of the time that Chris, Steph, and I devoted to strategy ultimately led us to do nothing. It's often the case that *intentionally deciding to do nothing is better than doing something.* But there were still "unknowns" that had the potential to trip us up. The biggest one turned out to be the involvement of the Indiana-based law firm, as they threatened to jeopardize everything we'd been working toward.

*Recognize the limits of judges.* As smart as judges are, they don't know everything, and they have varying degrees of numeracy (as revealed in their questioning and decisions). If they're to understand complex issues (like Medicare finance), it's smart to simplify those issues. In our brief submitted to the Court of Appeals, the hypothetical example devised by John Faust seemed to help the judges understand what was at stake. We all believed this was critical to their ruling in our favor.

*Uncontrolled egos can cause self-inflicted wounds and collateral damage.* Building a team of high-performing individuals probably means having a few large egos. The trick is leading and focusing those egos in a common direction for a common purpose at the appropriate time. Fortunately, this was the case with our team members (with a few exceptions).

*Details matter—particularly administrative details.* We could have been tripped up by paperwork snafus at many different stages throughout the case. We never were, thanks to many people, but my daughter Kristina's attention to detail was critically important.

*At the outset of any big initiative, make it clear who's in charge and, when necessary, provide reminders.* I typically consulted many members our team before doing anything, but when disagreements arose (as they inevitably did), everyone knew that I was the boss—something that was made clear in the agreement everyone signed.

*Don't get greedy.* This may be most important of all. We could have dickered with the DOJ over the size of the settlement, and it's possible we would have pried a little more money out of them. Then again, they could have responded by deciding to play hardball, which at the very least would have delayed the timing of the settlement and could have led to us getting less than what was originally agreed to. (We had a concern that HHS would lobby Congress to invalidate the court decision.) We concluded that seeking a larger settlement wasn't worth the risk.

The appeal process also reminded me of three rules that have applied to many different facets of my life:

**Rule 1:** Nothing is as easy as it seems. We originally thought we could a file appeals for between 100 and 125 hospitals and then wade through the administrative process, which we thought would cause the government to come to its senses and settle. We were wrong—*very* wrong.

**Rule 2:** Everything takes longer than planned. We had initially envisioned the appeal would be resolved in three years. The initial agreements with the hospitals ran from 2007 through 2009. But the appeal took much longer than we expected, which meant we needed to extend the agreements with all 730 hospitals, which was a real pain.

**Rule 3:** Things tend to get worse under pressure. As the appeal processes progressed, the other groups made our lives miserable with their misguided maneuvers. This brought a massive dose of added complexity and stress to our team. We had the lead, and now we had idiots messing us up.

In the end, the *Cape Cod* case was one of the largest appeals CMS has ever lost. The error totaled approximately $4 billion for the 2007–2011 years, for all hospitals nationally. Approximately $3 billion was paid to the hospitals that had filed appeals and were included in the initial settlement. (It is unclear whether and how much has been resolved for the remaining hospitals.) Winning the case and recovering the funds that rightfully belonged to the hospitals gave me the sensation that a race car driver must feel after winning the 24 Hours at Le Mans. It was a battle worth waging. And knowing what I know today, I'd do it all over again. The only thing I would change is losing Jayne.

# THE INTERSECTION OF THE INPATIENT PROSPECTIVE PAYMENT SYSTEM AND THE AREA WAGE INDEX

Created in 1983, the Inpatient Prospective Payment System (IPPS) is used to pay hospitals for inpatient services. The payment amounts are based in part on a wage adjustment known as the area wage index (AWI). The purpose of AWI is to adjust the standardized payment rate (a single rate for all hospitals nationally, which is varied by the type of case and other elements) for relative area wage differences. The adjustment is achieved using an AWI. To calculate the AWI, hospitals and their related wage data are grouped into geographic areas called CBSAs (Core Based Statistical Areas). An average hourly wage is calculated for each of those areas, which is divided by a national average hourly wage (developed from the same data) to create each area's index.

As an example of how the AWI works, and how it affects BN, consider a change made about twenty years ago. CMS removed from its wage data a collection of hospitals, known as "critical access hospitals," that tend to be small and serving rural communities. With wages at these hospitals typically lower than average, their removal from the wage data caused the national average hourly wage to rise and relative AWIs fell. (At this point absent any other adjustment, the hospitals would not be compensated for this decrease in relative AWIs.) Under a properly applied BN, as relative AWIs decreased, the BN adjustment factor to the rates would have increased. When applied to the payment rate, the monies that were theoretically lost in the wage adjustment were returned to the payment system via the increase in the payment rate [3 x 2 = 6 and 2 x 3 = 6]. The end result was that hospitals in aggregate recovered in the payment rate what they lost in the wage adjustment. In other words, they came out even.

# BUDGET NEUTRALITY (BN) EXPLAINED

When there are modifications to select parts of the Inpatient Prospective Payment System (IPPS), those modifications must be performed in a budget neutral manner. More specifically, any modifications should result in aggregate payments that are no more nor no less than the amount of the payments that would have been made had such changes not been made. Applicable areas are subject to a BN calculation, which is performed by CMS once each year for the areas required by statute to have such adjustments.

Under the IPPS, the payment for a patient's admission is based on the following factors:

- The national standardized rate that's paid for a specific procedure.
    - There are two elements of the standardized rate: the labor rate (primarily personnel costs) and the non-labor rate (everything else).

- Adjustments to the labor portion of the standardized rate for geographic labor cost differences, with those differences based on an area wage index (AWI).

- The area wage adjusted labor rate plus the non-labor rate is further adjusted for the case severity by a DRG (diagnosis-related group) weight, as well as other factors, not all of which are required to be budget neutral.

| Example | |
| --- | --- |
| National labor rate: | $3,000 |
| AWI | x1.10 |
| | =$3,300 |
| National non-labor rate: | +$1,000 |
| | =$4,300 |
| DRG weight | x 2.0 |
| Payment | =$8,600 |

The BN adjustment factor is calculated and applied nationally for all applicable geographic areas and hospitals for the particular types of adjustments that are the subject of the BN adjustment. Under the cumulative BN method, the BN factor and adjustment are permanently applied to the national standardized labor and non-labor payment rates that are the basis of payments to all IPPS hospitals. Several BN adjustments are combined into a single factor. As such, the BN adjustment for any annual reclassification of cases among the DRGs and annual changes in the DRG weights, annual changes in the AWI, and the annual application of the rural floor (RF) are all combined by the CMS into a single BN adjustment factor. (The RF-BN was calculated separately from fiscal year 2008 forward, mostly because of the error discussed in this book.)

Regardless of the national calculation and application of the BN adjustment, for this illustration the BN will be applied to only a single metropolitan statistical area (MSA) and assume that the only change between the years is the change in the adjustment for the change in the rural floor AWI.

| | Year 1 (FY 2005) | |
|---|---|---|
| **MSA "A"** | With RF AWI | 1.10 |
| | Without RF AWI | 1.00 |
| | AWI Differential | .10 |

Assume that this is the first year that MSA "A" becomes eligible for the rural floor (RF). Since this is the first year of the area's qualification for the RF AWI, the payment effect of the ten percentage point difference in the AWI under the cumulative method is permanently removed from the standardized payment rate via the BN factor. This would reduce the standardized payment rate for all hospitals to compensate for the additional dollars that will flow to the MSA "A" hospitals, by virtue of receiving payments based on the higher AWI. Since this is permanently reduced from the standardized rate, no further adjustment should be necessary for this ten percentage point difference in the AWI, unless there is a future change in RF payments.

| Year 2 (FY 2006) | | |
|---|---|---|
| **MSA "A"** | With RF AWI | 1.11 |
| | Without RF AWI | 1.00 |
| | AWI Differential | .11 |

In this year, while there is a slight change is the RF AWIs, CMS repeated the same calculation. Under the CMS applied BN methodology, the effect of the 11 percentage point difference in the AWI was removed via the BN adjustment factor. What should have been removed is only the effect for the difference between the FY 2006 "With RF AWI" (see entry above) and FY 2005 "With RF AWI" (see entry above) or a one percentage point difference. Thus, the CMS method duplicates in FY 2006 the ten percentage point difference that has already been permanently removed in FY 2005.

# YEAR 3 (FY 2007)

Assume that the FY 2007 "With RF AWI" (1.11) is the same as the FY 2006 "With RF AWI" (1.11) and the FY 2007 "Without RF AWI" (1.00) is also the same as in FY 2006. When CMS performed the same calculation for FY 2007 as it did in FY 2006, it will again remove from the standardized payment rate the eleven percentage point difference in the RF AWIs, which it has already removed in FY 2005 and FY 2006 for the previous FYs (nothing additional should have been removed).

Therefore, under this approach, the FY 2005 BN factor permanently removed the ten percentage point AWI difference. It was removed again in the FY 2006 BN factor, and then again in the FY 2007 BN factor. This means that the same effect has been removed two additional times (in FY 2006 and FY 2007, plus the additional one percentage point for FY 2007). The CMS approach thereby duplicated the BN effect for all fiscal years following the first year of the applicability of the RF AWI to the particular area. In other words, BN was being implemented in a "budget negative" manner.

# HOW ADVOCACY— AND BENEFIT CHANGES—CAUSED A FEDERAL PROGRAM TO EXPLODE IN SIZE

On January 1, 1940, the federal government established the Old-Age and Survivors Insurance (OASI) Trust Fund as a separate account in the United States Treasury. And on August 1, 1956, the federal government established the Federal Disability Insurance (DI) Trust Fund as another separate account in the Treasury. These funds, which make up the Social Security Trust Fund, conduct the financial operations of the OASI and DI programs. These funds have seen significant growth in costs, which reflects a rise in the number of beneficiaries. They're cautionary tales about what happens when federal benefit programs face pressures to expand eligibility (sometimes referred to as "mission creep").

While inflows to these funds are relatively defined—driven by the economic growth, the numbers of people employed, relative salary levels, etc.—outflows are variable and determined by the number of eligible retirees/recipients and the number of those eligible for disability payments. When these outflow variables grow more rapidly, the result is deficits (annual and long term) in the funds. Therefore, higher levels of economic growth generally will have a positive effect on the trust funds if the outflow variables do not change as rapidly. Conversely, economic slowdowns can accelerate increases in those eligible for payments, e.g., some people may decide to retire earlier and begin to draw payments. Understanding these effects will help bring clarity to the status of these funds and how they change.

The primary receipts of these two funds come from payroll tax contributions (Social Security taxes). Federal law requires that all employees who work in OASDI-covered employment, and their employers, make payroll tax contributions on their wages. Self-employed persons must make payroll tax contributions on their covered net earnings from self-employment.

The U.S. Treasury initially deposits payroll tax contributions into the trust funds each month on an estimated basis. Subsequently, the Treasury makes adjustments based on the certified amount of wages and self-employment earnings in the records of the Social Security Administration.

Now let's concentrate on the Disability Insurance (DI) Trust Fund.

**Description of the DI benefit:** Since 1957, the DI portion of the OASI Trust Fund has been paying monthly benefits to disabled children (aged eighteen and over) of retired and deceased workers if the disability began before age eighteen. The age by which disability must have begun was later changed to twenty-two. And since 1968, the OASI Trust Fund has been paying reduced monthly benefits to disabled widows and widowers at ages fifty and over. In 1991, the standards for what qualified as a disability of the widow or widower were liberalized.

In 2017, about 10.5 million individuals were receiving monthly benefits from the OASI Trust Fund because of their disabilities or the disabilities of children, up from 522,000 in 1960.* In 2017, the OASI Trust Fund paid out nearly $143 billion to the people described above.[†]

**Indexing of the DI Trust Fund:** Benefits from the trust funds are usually indexed. This is supposed to enable the benefits to keep pace with inflation, though there is no guarantee that they will, as the benefits typically fluctuate based on national economic growth rates. The biggest driving force of increased outlays from these funds is the growth in the number of individuals who are eligible to receive fund benefits.

**DI benefit eligibility:** The DI eligibility was initially targeted at those individuals who were physically disabled and unable to work. Thus, these individuals were deemed to need some form of cash assistance. The DI benefit was designed to provide these individuals with a subsistence level of cash, since they were unable to provide for themselves.

**Evolution of the application industry:** In order to obtain DI benefits, individuals have needed to know how to apply for them. That led some enterprising individuals to start firms that help

* https://www.ssa.gov/OACT/TR/2018/IV_B_LRest.html#493869

† https://www.ssa.gov/OACT/TR/2018/III_A_cyoper.html#985713—Table III. A5.—Distribution of Benefit Payments by Type of Beneficiary or Payment, Calendar Years 2016 and 2017

people traverse the complex application system and the complex rules. These firms would also help those individuals appeal if their application was denied. Over time, these applicant firms blossomed into an industry that sought benefits for people on a contingency basis—the firm would not get paid unless the individual attained the benefit. Thus, some firms got paid based on a percentage of the benefit attained, rather than merely a flat fee. The growth of these firms contributed to a growth in the number of DI beneficiaries, and that has complicated the job of actuaries, who estimate how a program will grow over time. They model using an "induction factor," which refers to the way in which the creation of a program—or subsequent rule changes to the program—often "induce" behaviors that increase program outlays. But the existence of the enrollment-driven firms often renders these projections wildly inaccurate.

Along the way, there were advocates who would help people with other types of disabilities (other than the physically disabled) secure DI benefits. Over time, a wide variety of individuals have been made eligible. Today, individuals who have ADHD and ADD are getting cash assistance, regardless of their financial status or their family's financial status. In 2018, nearly $8.2 billion in benefits were directed to children, and about $536 million to husbands and wives. Another $135 billion went to disabled workers.*

Also, qualification for cash assistance is a gateway into getting benefits under the Medicare Program—another trust fund. So, all of the individuals who get DI benefits also likely are entitled to Medicare benefits for their health insurance. For someone aged twenty, for example, taxpayers could be paying for their health-

* https://www.ssa.gov/OACT/STATS/table4a6.html

care benefits for decades, as well as paying them cash assistance. Many of these individuals are healthy, other than their ADD.

**Growth in DI beneficiaries:** There has been an explosion in the DI program's outlays. The application companies are partly responsible for this, but the primary driver has been the expansion of eligibility. In 1960, there were 155,000 disabled children receiving $48 million in DI benefits. In 2018, benefits were going to nearly 1.1 million children, at a cost of nearly $8.2 billion.* Much of this explosive growth in outlays is directly linked to the explosive increase in eligible children, which in turn is directly linked to the expansion of the eligibility criteria and the related definition. This has caused the DI trust fund to go further into deficit status, and the trustees have diverted funds from the OASI portion of the OASDI TF to keep the DI portion solvent. And that has put more and more pressure on the OASI portion of the fund in the process. For benefit adjudicators, it's easier to say "yes" than it is to say "no."

While the expansion of eligibility initially seemed like a good idea, it has mutated over time into something different. While some people needed expanded eligibility, such expansions have led to a cost increase no one could have anticipated and likely would have rejected had the actual costs been known.

---

* https://www.ssa.gov/OACT/STATS/table4a6.html

# SOLICITATION OF HOSPITALS

*The material below is a generic version of the document we sent to hospitals we were recruiting to join the appeal.*

TGC, LLC
Health Policy and Regulatory Consultants

P.O. Box XXX
Highland, MD XXXXX
Phone: 301.854.XXXX
Fax: 301.854.XXXX

By E-Mail

March 1, 2007

Mr. John Doe
Vice President of Finance
Anywhere Hospital
111 Washington Street
Suite 101
Baltimore, Maryland   21244

Dear Mr. Doe:

We appreciate the opportunity to submit this proposal to Anywhere Hospital (Provider Number 00-0000) located in Baltimore, Maryland. The proposal involves services related to an issue in the Budget Neutrality (BN) calculation utilized by the Medicare program for the acute care payment system as it relates to the rural floor.

# BACKGROUND

The Medicare program pays for acute inpatient services through a Prospective Payment System (PPS). The PPS utilizes payment rates that are adjusted by various factors to develop the applicable payment. Annually, the Medicare program makes changes to the payment variables some of which are required to be made in a BN manner. T. Giovanis & Company (TGC) has discovered an error in the BN method and data related to how the BN adjustment is calculated and incorporates the effect of the rural floor. The error results in an inappropriate reducing effect on the standardized payment rate and therefore payments to PPS hospitals. The method and manner in which these adjustments are made results in a duplication in years after the initial year of application of the rural floor of all or a portion of the adjustment. This issue is the subject of this engagement proposal.

## PURPOSE OF THE ENGAGEMENT

There exists in the acute care PPS a set of payment rates. These rates are understated because of the method and variables utilized by the Medicare program to calculate the BN adjustment. This adjustment is applied to the otherwise applicable payment rates and can have an increasing or decreasing effect on the rates. The nature of this engagement is to appeal a series of cost reporting periods and/or Federal fiscal years in order to secure additional payments for the participating hospitals. Because this effect has occurred over a period of time, this effort will involve both retrospective and prospective elements. Accordingly, there will be appeals filed on behalf of participating hospitals that could potentially cover 5-6 cost reporting periods and/or Federal fiscal years.

## NATURE OF THE ISSUE

Annually, the Medicare program makes several changes to the payment variables in the system. When the Medicare program calculates the BN adjustment for any particular year it attempts to assure that aggregate payments are no more nor no less than what those payments would have been had the change in the payment system variables not been made.

In the process of making the BN adjustment for the area wage index, particularly as it relates to the rural floor, the approach utilized by Medicare causes a duplicating effect in the BN adjustment and therefore in the rates. The BN effect of the method utilized is appropriate for the first year where the rural floor is applicable to a state or hospitals. However, in the second and subsequent years the method duplicates all or part of the BN effect that has already been removed in the first year of applicability. This situation is created by several elements one of which is the fact that the BN factors are permanently included into the payment rate and are not subsequently removed.

The error does not affect the level or applicability of the rural floor itself. Rather it relates to the measurement of the cost of the floor and the related reduction in the payment rates and aggregate payments. Therefore, this reduced effect applies to all PPS hospitals and represents a net reduction in total PPS payments.

# APPROACH

This issue will likely be resolved through the filing of appeals with the PRRB (Provider Reimbursement Review Board) and ultimately ruled upon by the courts. The law firm of Vinson & Elkins has been engaged to pursue this appeal effort. At our request this firm has already performed legal research and has determined that this issue can be appealed.

As previously mentioned, we foresee the filing of appeals for a variety of hospital cost reporting periods and/or Federal fiscal years, the specific years that are filed and their sequencing will be determined at our option. In the end, we believe that there could be 5-6 years from 2004 through 2009 that could be under appeal. Depending on the particular year, appeals could be filed by filing within 180 days of the final rule for that Federal fiscal year or by filing within 180 days of the respective cost reporting period NPR (Notice of Program Reimbursement).

Any successful resolution of this issue will have a prospective effect in that the PPS rates would be increased for the understatement that is implicit in them. Both retrospective and prospective effects would be requested in the appeals that are filed.

As part of the appeal process certain data will be needed from each hospital. At this time we do not envision that this data would be extensive and would likely be data that the hospital would have readily available, such as copies of various NPRs, copies of settled (or filed) Medicare cost report pages, a proportioning of hospital discharges/payments among various Federal fiscal years and other information of this type.

# DUTIES AND RESPONSIBILITIES

**Duties of TGC**

TGC will perform or cause to be performed such duties as needed to resolve this issue. These duties are expected to include:

- Engage appropriate legal counsel
- Provide general overall direction to the appeal process
- Oversee and/or participate in obtaining applicable data from the participating hospitals

- Perform estimates of the aggregate effect of the BN error for various fiscal years
- Determine the years for which appeal will be filed and their sequencing
- Work directly with or assist legal counsel in the development and prosecution of the appeal(s)
- Perform the preliminary estimates of the impact of the BN effect for each participating hospital
- Work with legal counsel on strategy and other issues related to the Medicare program
- Work with, briefing and preparing expert witnesses, as needed
- Work, as needed, on data issues for the appeal(s)
- Provide periodic updates of the status of the appeal and related activities
- Seek resolution of the appeal(s) at TGC's discretion based upon advice of counsel
- Assure timely payment of legal and other appeal related fees
- Work on other issues that may arise

# DUTIES OF THE PARTICIPATING HOSPITAL

The hospital will perform the following duties.
- Sign an engagement letter with TGC
- Designate a contact individual for the hospital
- Provide data and information in a form and format specified by TGC or legal counsel by the deadline specified by TGC
- Sign an engagement letter with the law firm and designate that

firm as the hospital's representative on this issue
- Work with legal counsel and TGC should any issue need to be transferred to and/or from any existing appeal to the group appeal for this issue
- Review updates on the appeal effort
- Respond as needed with other information as requested by the specified deadline
- Timely notify TGC of any payment by Medicare resulting from this effort
- Pay the applicable fees as indicated in the fees section of the agreement
- Otherwise participate in the appeals and provide data as needed

# ENGAGEMENT TIMING AND FEES

### Engagement Timing

There will be a series of years appealed which may include years from 2004 through 2009 (as determined by TGC). There will be a prospective effect related to this effort as the appeals will ask that Medicare correct the error for the years appealed and then fix the error prospectively from some point forward. Currently, under the approach envisioned we have filed an initial Federal FY 2007 (fiscal year) appeal for a group(s) of hospitals at the end of January 2007. For strategic reasons the appeal group that is moved forward may be composed of a small group of participating hospitals or all participating hospitals. If strategically a small group is selected then individual appeals or another group appeal(s) would be utilized for the remaining participating hospitals some of which may be filed after the initial group. All participating hospitals at that time will be included in an FY 2007 appeal.

Thereafter, for these initial hospitals and other hospitals signed too late for the FY 2007 initial appeal(s), we would determine the year(s) that are within 180 days of the respective NPRs (Notices of Program Reimbursement) and then initiate the process of filing an appeal for the earliest applicable year, which is anticipated to be FY 2004. It is possible that based on the amounts in controversy that we would choose not to pursue years earlier than FY 2004.

Years after FY 2004 would be pursued in sequence as those NPRs become available and appeals would be filed for FY 2008 and FY 2009 based upon the date of publication of those applicable final rules. Ultimately, there will likely be hospitals added to the initial FY 2007 appeal (or a separate but similar group appeal) as the applicable NPRs are available for those hospitals not included in the original filing for that year. In all, it is anticipated that there could be 5–6 years under appeal potentially including years from FY 2004 through FY 2009.

Because of the timing sensitivity, hospitals should provide the FY 2007 data listed on Attachments I - III as soon as possible. Similar data will be requested separately for all other years for which appeals may be filed.

# ENGAGEMENT FEES

The fee structure for this engagement will have two components: a performance fee and a fixed fee per hospital, both of which are payable only if the appeal(s) is/are successful or TGC is successful in reaching a settlement with the Federal government.

**Performance Fee:** Within each year there are two components to the error effect: the effect from the immediately preceding year to the current year and the accumulation of prior year effect both of which are being appealed. Under this fee component the hospital will pay a performance fee equal to 25 percent of the increase in payment resulting from a successful appeal or settlement. It is possible that there could be either a prospective resolution or correction forward and/or there could be a retrospective resolution. If there is a successful resolution, the fee will be based on the increased payment effect for the years included in the successful resolution either by way of appeal or negotiated settlement with the Federal government. The increase in payments would have a flow through effect on other payments to the hospital, such as disproportionate share and indirect medical education payments (which would be requested in the appeals) and increases in those payments would also be subject to the performance fee. It is important that hospital be included in the appeal of all years through the point of correction in the event there is a resolution of the appeal on this issue. An appeal would not be filed for any year in which the error effect is fully corrected.

**Fixed Fee:** Under this component, in addition to the performance fee, there would be a fixed fee per hospital for recovering the costs of pursuing the appeal. This fixed fee would be in the amount of $10,000 per hospital and would be added to the applicable performance fees.

Both the performance fee and the fixed fee would only be payable if the appeal effort results in a successful resolution either through the PRRB, CMS administrative relief, a positive court determination or a settlement agreement with the Federal government. In no case would the hospital pay more than it received as a result of the appeal effort.

The fees would be payable upon invoicing. Such invoicing would not occur until the hospital has been paid. The hospital will be responsible for notifying TGC when it receives any applicable settlement payments from Medicare. Fees payable would be due within 30 days of invoicing. It is possible that invoicing would occur and the fees would be payable as the years are settled.

Hospitals that participate in this appeal effort agree to keep the terms of this agreement confidential.

# RIGHT TO RESOLVE APPEAL(S) AND RIGHT TO DETERMINE TO CEASE THE APPEAL EFFORTS

This appeal effort involves issues that are both legally and technically complex. Due to these complexities and the risk free nature of the fee structure, the hospital by agreeing to participate in these appeal(s) efforts coveys to TGC the sole discretion to resolve or settle this issue for any and all of the appealed years either at the PRRB, administrative hearings, court level or negotiations with the Federal government through its designated representatives. Such resolution would be based on the circumstances and advice of counsel at the point of such resolution.

TGC has arranged for the capital to fund the appeal effort. TGC is obligated for the repayment of this capital and is expending its own resources. In consideration that TGC is therefore the principal funding source for this effort TGC in its sole discretion shall retain the right to choose to terminate these appeal efforts including a determination as to whether the initial appeal effort should move forward which will depend on whether a critical mass of hospitals participate. Such determination may be based in part on the advice of counsel but the advice of such counsel is not required for such determination.

# TIMING SENSITIVITY AND DEADLINE

By agreeing to participate in this appeal the hospital recognizes that there are specific timing sensitivities related to the filing of the appeals involved. The hospital understands that it will be its responsibility to provide the needed data and information for the filing of the related appeals. It is the hospital's responsibility to assure that the data and information is received by TGC by the dates and times that are specified by TGC. The hospital through its participation understands that every effort will be made by TGC and legal counsel to insure that the hospital is included in the respective appeal years. However, by the hospital's participation it agrees to hold TGC and legal counsel harmless for the lack of receipt and/or the related lack of the inclusion of the hospital in any appeal year.

To be included in the next series of appeal(s) by March 21, 2007, the hospital must submit: a signed engagement letter with TGC; the hospitals contact individuals information (Attachment I); the hospitals FY 2007 data (Attachment III); have returned to us a signed representation letter designating the law firm as its designated representative on this issue (Attachment II), and have signed an engagement letter with legal counsel. Hospitals missing this deadline may participate but will be included in other FFY 2007 appeals and/or appeals developed based upon the hospital's NPR dates.

Once the hospital's contact information is received that individual will be sent the engagement letter by legal counsel.

# CONFIDENTIALITY OF APPEAL INFORMATION

The hospital acknowledges that TGC has invested considerable time, resources and legal costs related to the issue that is the subject of these appeal efforts. As part of participating in the group effort, the hospital acknowledges that it may become aware or be provided with information that represents intellectual property of TGC as it relates to this issue including any evidentiary type information. By the hospital's participation it acknowledges the existence of such information and agrees to hold in confidence such information and will not otherwise divulge such information to any other providers, firms or persons other than those that are a party to these appeals or have made a similar acknowledgement as to the confidentially of such information.

# FIRM QUALIFICATIONS

TGC is a broad based reimbursement policy and reimbursement firm specializing in the Medicare and Medicaid arenas. The firm has participated in successful legislative, regulatory, and reimbursement strategies on behalf of its clients since 1990. The firm has developed specialized reimbursement strategies and techniques, which it has successfully employed on behalf of its clients with the result of increasing payments.

The firm has health policy expertise that has allowed it to develop payment methodologies for various types of payment systems such as acute care and long term care payment systems and others. It is TGC's broad policy experiences and expertise as well as techniques that allow it to understand and identify unique issues such as the issue that is the subject of the appeal effort.

Additional information about our firm and its experiences and expertise can be found at: www.tgiovanis.com.

The above presents the issues and approaches regarding the BN appeal opportunity as well as the terms and conditions for the hospitals participation. If after reviewing this proposal you have any questions, please contact us to discuss any question you may have. Alternatively, if your hospital desires to participate in the appeal(s) please signify such agreement to participate and acceptance of the terms of this proposal by executing and returning a copy of this proposal to us along with the data need for this appeal effort.

For the Hospital

Accepted By:

Date

For TGC, LLC

Accepted By:

**Theodore Giovanis**

Date

Attachments

Attachment I – Hospital Contact Information

Attachment II – Representation Letter

Attachment III – Hospital Medicare Payment Information

# ATTACHMENT I

Budget Neutrality Appeal
Hospital Contact Information

Proper Name of Hospital:

Hospital Medicare Provider Number:

Hospital Address:
Street:
City/State/ZIPCode:
County of Hospital Location:

Hospital Contact Individual Information:

Contact Name:
Contact Title:
Address: (if different from Hospital)
E-mail Address:
Telephone Number:
Fax Number:

Hospital Fiscal Year End Month and Day:__/__/

Fiscal Intermediary:

Affiliation/Chain Membership/Related Hospital Information:

Does your hospital operate under common ownership or control with another hospital (or hospital's)?
Yes _____ No _____

If yes, please provide the name of the chain or controlling
entity. _____

If unsure, please contact TGC either at the e-mail addresses
below or 301-854-XXXX

E-mail this Attachment to:

# ATTACHMENT II

Budget Neutrality Appeal
Representation Letter

[ON HOSPITAL LETTERHEAD]

March __, 2007

Suzanne Cochran, Esq., Chairman
Provider Reimbursement Review Board
2520 Lord Baltimore Drive
Suite L
Baltimore, Maryland 21244-2670

Re:  Appointment of Representative
              [Name of Hospital]
Provider No. [##-####]
FFY 2007 Wage Index Appeal

Dear Ms. Cochran:

[Name of Hospital], Provider No. [##-####], hereby appoints
Vinson & Elkins L.L.P. to serve as the provider's representative in its appeal of the federal fiscal year 2007 wage
index issue.  Please direct all correspondence regarding this
appeal to the attention of:

Christopher L. Keough
Vinson & Elkins L.L.P.
1455 Pennsylvania Avenue, NW
Suite 600
Washington, DC  20004

Sincerely,

# POST-SETTLEMENT EMAIL TO HOSPITALS

Once the federal government began paying the hospitals in our appeal group, we started sending emails to our contacts at those hospitals to collect the funds we were owed, as part of our original agreement. Reproduced below is a generic example of the email sent to the hospitals.

From:
[mailto:]
Sent: Wednesday, May 23, 2012 5:27 PM
To:
Subject: RF BN Appeals – Pre Invoicing Notification

On or before May 25, 2012, your hospital should receive payment (or an off set to a liability owed to Medicare in which case the TGC fees still apply) from Medicare of the settlement amount for the Rural Floor (RF) Budget Neutrality (BN) settlement for your hospital.

As the hospital's designated contact individual, you will

separately be receiving the invoice (and related information) for the TGC, LLC fees for the RF BN settlement as per
the agreement between TGC and the hospital. We ask that
you route this invoice through the hospital processes for
making payment to TGC. The TGC fee includes all applicable fees including the fees for legal counsel on this matter.
The invoice you will receive will be for all services inclusive.

The invoicing e-mail will be sent from the following e-mail
address, so please assure that this address is in your address
book. This e-mail address should be the address to which you
should communicate any invoicing related questions. (For
invoicing, TGC will be using the invoicing process of XXX.
XXX, who is the office manager at XXX, will be managing
the invoicing process for TGC for the RF BN settlement.)

The invoicing e-mail will include a file containing the following three documents all included in one PDF file:

- the TGC invoice;
- the TGC tax information including a W-9; and
- instructions for making payment to TGC.

All of the above are intended to facilitate prompt payment
to TGC.

Please remember that TGC and its legal team have pursued
this issue since 2007 on behalf of the TGC hospitals and
throughout that time there have been no fees paid to TGC
by any hospital; therefore prompt payment is appreciated.

Change of Ownership (CHOW) hospitals. The total settlement amount covers all years appealed by TGC and will be paid to the current holder of the Medicare provider number. Therefore, if there was a CHOW during the period to which the settlement amount applies and depending on the nature of the CHOW, the hospital may need to contact the new or prior owner and work out the details of the apportionment of the settlement amount and TGC fees. TGC has not apportioned the fees. Each hospital's invoice indicates the hospital's entire aggregate settlement amount for the years appealed by TGC and total fees owed to TGC which may apply to different owners. TGC should receive its fees in a single payment and the hospital will need to work out any fee allocation related details.

Booking or Recording of the Settlement and Fees. Hospitals should note that when booking or recording the RF BN settlement amounts, the fees owed to TGC need to be considered. The TGC invoices for its fees will be sent shortly. Thus, hospitals could wait to record the settlement and related fees until they receive the TGC invoice for fees (or may choose to estimate the fees if desired) which will allow the recording of the net settlement amount.

We will not be providing the TGC fee estimates at this point; hospitals should wait until they receive their formal invoice.

Thank you.

# GLOSSARY

- **Admission:** An inpatient admission to an acute general hospital.

- **Area Wage Index (AWI):** An adjustment to a Medicare rate for the relative difference in labor costs across geographic areas.

- **Budget Neutrality (BN):** A process used in rate setting when making changes to select payment variables. It is intended to ensure that once such variables are changed, aggregate payments are no more nor no less than the amount of the payments that would have occurred had such changes not been made. Thus, budget neutrality is inherently redistributive across hospitals.

- **Diagnosis Related Group (DRG):** A grouping system used to categorize patients for payment or measurement in an acute general hospital.

- **Discharge:** A patient formally released from the hospital by a medical practitioner.

- **Inpatient Prospective Payment System (IPPS):** A payment system introduced in 1983 that pays inpatient acute care hospitals based on a standardized payment rate that is adjusted by select variables differentiating hospital discharges by classifying those discharges into diagnosis related groups (DRGs).

- **Laspeyres Index:** A mathematical approach used in rate setting and other policy endeavors; used by the Medicare program to achieve budget neutrality.

- **Medicaid:** The federal program that covers inpatient and outpatient services for the poor, as well as long-term care services for the elderly.

- **Medicare:** The federal program for, generally, the elderly that covers inpatient and outpatient services.

- **Notice of Program Reimbursement (NPR):** A notification to a Medicare provider of services that signals the final administrative determination of payments due to the provider for that provider's fiscal year. The notification usually comes after the hospital's cost report has been audited or reviewed by the government, which is typically about two calendar years after the end of the respective hospital's fiscal year. The date of issue of the NPR signals the beginning of the period during which a hospital may appeal that year, which is generally limited to 180 calendar days from the NPR date.

- **Provider Reimbursement Review Board (PRRB):** The administrative appeal body where all Medicare appeals by providers must originate.

- **Rural Floor:** A statutory provision requiring that no urban hospital in a state be paid less than the rural hospitals in that state, which essentially increases the payments to the affected urban hospitals.